How to Lead in CHURCH CONFLICT

Healing Ungrieved Loss

How to Lead in
CHURCH
CONFLICT
Healing Ungrieved Loss

K. Brynolf Lyon and Dan P. Moseley

Abingdon Press
Nashville

HOW TO LEAD IN CHURCH CONFLICT
HEALING UNGRIEVED LOSS

Copyright © 2012 by Abingdon Press

This book is printed on acid-free paper.

Library of Congress Cataloging-in-Publication Data

Lyon, K. Brynolf, 1953–
    How to lead in church conflict : healing ungrieved loss / K. Brynolf Lyon and Dan P. Moseley.
        p. cm.
    Includes bibliographical references (p.   ).
    ISBN 978-1-4267-4233-0 (book - pbk. / trade pbk. : alk. paper) 1. Conflict management—Religious aspects—Christianity. 2. Church controversies. I. Moseley, Dan. II. Title.
    BV652.9.L88 2012
    253—dc23

                                                                                2011048444

12 13 14 15 16 17 18 19 20 21—10 9 8 7 6 5 4 3 2 1

MANUFACTURED IN THE UNITED STATES OF AMERICA

Contents

CHAPTER 1

Leading in Conflict:
An Introduction to the Issues

*Our words are too fragile. God's silence is too deep. But oh,
what gorgeous sounds our failures make: words flung against the
silence like wine glasses pitched against a hearth. As lovely as they
are, they were meant for smashing. For when they do, it is as if
a little of God's own music breaks through.*
—*Barbara Brown Taylor*

The voice on the other end of the line was controlled and measured. "Bishop, we are in trouble. There is a group in the church that is threatening to leave if we don't get rid of our minister. We have tried to deal with it, but it is getting worse. Can you come and talk with us?"

These calls are becoming more frequent in churches in the first part of the twenty-first century. Conflict among members of churches seems to be escalating. Bishops and other middle judicatory leaders report to us that they are spending more and more of their time helping congregations deal with conflict. Tensions overflow, and anger flares as people seem to be unable to sort out their differences in ways that promise a positive future.

This is a time in the publishing world during which dozens of books are available for helping churches deal with conflict.[1] The past fifty years have seen the growth of a conflict-resolution

1

industry that has produced theories and consultants by the skid-full to help congregations and other organizations when they confront a major conflict. New techniques for helping congregations resolve their differences are published regularly.

But even with all the expert help available for dealing with conflict, it sometimes seems to be getting worse, rather than better. Of course, when we look at the biblical witness, we observe that when humans sought to understand themselves in relationship to the work of God in the world, they seemed to be in a continual state of conflict. Our early faith stories reveal humans who seem to be at odds with the desires of their God and one another. Adam and Eve wanted more knowledge than God wanted them to have. Humans wanted access to the heavens and built a tower, only to have it destroyed and their language confused. The people of Israel were at odds with God's desires when they assumed their election was about their privilege rather than their responsibility to live just and compassionate lives.

Even the presence of Jesus in the world brought conflict to those around him. His witness to God's life in the world resulted in conflict within the community of faith that formed and nurtured him. As the church moved out of its community of formation into the larger world, people who embraced his Spirit were in constant conflict among themselves as to the meaning of his life for them. Additionally, the church that the Spirit of Jesus formed was in conflict with the values of the power structures that sought to control the lives of the citizens. The church itself has even lost sight of its God and become an oppressive, conflictual force in the lives of others. Everywhere we look, including in the church, conflict seems to be an inextricable part of human life generally, as well as the lives of those who would seek to discover and bear witness to the Spirit of God in the world.

Conflict is an essential part of what it is to be human. It is not in and of itself sinful. The problem, in other words, is not that we have conflicts but how we deal with the conflicts we inevitably have. At its core, conflict is about how we treat one another as we process—and fail to process—the losses and blessings of our lives. The thesis of this book is that leading congregations in intense conflict is, in its deepest dimensions, about helping congregations grieve loss.

Although this may seem like a simple proposition, it is really quite complex. By learning to *more fully* engage the losses evoked in conflict and to be present to them in ways that open us to their deeper, more ambiguous meanings, congregations will have greater opportunity to discover the transforming power of conflict.

This book does not add to the literature that offers new techniques to help resolve conflict. Instead, it invites the reader into a deeper analysis of the nature of groups in conflict, with the hope that the reader might gain insight into ways that she or he can be faithfully present within a conflict and discover a kind of leadership that helps the conflict itself produce transforming power. A deeper understanding of the theological nature of conflict and of the way groups of people tend to react will enable congregational members and ministers to wind their way toward hopeful outcomes.

This book therefore is not so much a "how-to" book for dealing with conflict in congregations as it is a "how-to-be-here" book for those who wish to create a space in which the conflicts, losses, and blessings of life can be held together in community before God, allowing the Spirit to move in troubling but ultimately vitalizing ways among us. We believe that when this is done, congregations might have a greater chance of deepening their spiritual lives and enhancing their witness to the God who offers abundant life to the world. We believe that leadership in congregations should be conceived in such a way as to help create spaces of reverie in which persons can reflect prayerfully about their lives as gifts from God, who works through constant change, loss, and blessing to bring into existence a transformed world. We believe that both lay and clergy leaders who have a deep understanding of the complex and chaotic reality of vital life, and who can situate it within the spiritual discipline of learning from experience embedded within the liturgical life of the church, can gain insight into how they might become a holding and birthing presence for such creative vitality in the midst of conflict.

The prophet Ezekiel encourages the people of Israel with the promise of God to restore the dispersed to their home (Ezekiel 11:19). The promise includes the gift of a "heart of flesh" rather than a heart of stone. We believe that this is the kind of change of heart required for leaders of congregations in conflict. A heart of flesh is one that is vulnerable and deeply empathic. It is one that fully experiences the reality of the situation and feels the threat and the possibility of sharp differences within the congregation. In this book we will develop insights that will help a congregational leader be fully present to individuals and groups who struggle to discover their future. With the understandings and insights available in this book, leaders will discover that hearts sometimes develop stonelike qualities in conflict, but those hearts can be replaced with hearts of flesh and can contribute to healing and transformation for the future.

The psychoanalyst Erik Erikson once wrote that psychotherapists must develop a "disciplined subjectivity" in order to be present in the messiness of the therapeutic relationship in helpful ways.[2] Such discipline emerges from the hard work of study, the therapists' own therapy experience, and learning from the practice of therapy itself. This book is our effort to contribute to that process for pastors and laypersons, to provide resources for disciplining the subjective presence they bring to ministry within their congregations, as well as the *intersubjective* spaces cocreated between the pastor and members. For it is finally here that God is served for better or worse. The challenge we confront is how to discipline our inner and relational worlds well so that we might be able to learn how to form leadership in conflict fruitfully. But what does that mean?

Some Important Things about Leadership

The revisioning required to engage conflict well begins with the very idea of leadership itself. In other words, to lead well in conflict is not just a matter of applying some well-worn notion of leadership to conflict situations. We must rethink the nature of leadership itself. In order to get at our understanding of leadership, James Burns's classic definition of leadership is a helpful foil. We will use Burns's definition to point in the direction of the issues that will recur throughout this book. Burns indicates that "leadership over human beings is exercised when persons with certain motives and purposes mobilize, in competition or conflict with others, institutional, political, psychological, and other resources so as to arouse, engage, and satisfy the motives of the followers . . . Leadership is exercised in a condition of conflict or competition in which leaders contend in appealing to the motive bases of potential followers."[3] This definition assumes that conflict is an inherent dimension of leadership. It emerges in a situation of competing interests. Leadership, from Burns's perspective, inevitably arises in a situation in which competing beliefs, desires, and fears are present in the group. Although conflict does not exhaust the domain of leadership for Burns, it is certainly an essential component shaping leadership.

From our perspective, Burns is correct to note the inherent dimension of conflict in leadership. Group life, we say, is characterized by a multiplicity or diversity in response to which the leadership function in the group coconstructs a way ahead. The leadership that develops may be good or bad, but either way, the leadership guides the group in relation to its diversity or competing interests. If a congregation, for example, seeks to be faithful to some vision of what it believes God might be calling it to be or do, then there is some distance between where it is and where it wants to be. Congregational members often have differing ideas about that distance and destination. If the church is called to participate in the emerging reign of God, yet what is emerging is perceived to be better or different than what is, there is conflict. How God's reign is to be expressed and lived out is not always clear when seen through the eyes of different people. Therefore, there are likely to be conflicts between goals and strategies that are suggested to move the church from where it is to a more loving or just way of living in the world. Sorting through the various reasons and motives of the members in order to determine what strategies might best guide the group's activities requires leadership to navigate the differences and to manage the conflicts that arise because of those differences.

Burns also defines leadership as "inducing followers to act for certain goals that represent the values and motivations—the wants and needs, the aspirations and expectations—of both leaders and followers. The genius of leadership lies in the manner in which leaders see and act on their own and their followers' values and motivations."[4] The leaders and followers are in this together. They affect one another and shape one another. In an even stronger sense than that implied by Burns, however, we believe that groups select, shape, and construct their followers and leaders. The uniqueness of groups helps form the uniqueness of their leaders. Leading groups is different in each situation and each context. The hopes and dreams, the fears and anxieties of members will affect what kind of leadership is required and produced by the group. Groups call forth certain gifts of leadership depending on their unique circumstance and their desired purpose or goal. Again, it is important to be aware here that the gifts of leadership that the group thinks it wants may be good or bad, helpful or unhelpful in relation to its overt, primary purpose. Our claim, however, is simply that leadership and followership emerge together in congregational life.

Leadership, then, is not best understood as something done by a person but as an emotional function that emerges within the vitality of group life, many dimensions of which are beyond our conscious awareness and control.[5] That leadership becomes embodied in certain persons (pastors, lay people, and so on) should not obscure our awareness that leading is a group function. We should not talk, as Burns does, about "leadership over human beings" but rather about the way "the group 'co-creates' leaders and followers who, in a mutual, reciprocal interchange, serve conscious and unconscious purposes for the group."[6] In this perspective on group life, the leader is not the singular hero (or villain) who rides into town to straighten out or command his or her followers. The classic notion of the leader as a "self contained ego making conscious, rational choices based upon 'real world' contingencies" is radically deconstructed from the perspective we are developing in this book.[7]

When we talk about "the leader" in this book, we are talking about someone who is being authorized by the group to perform a particular role on its behalf, whereas when we talk about "leadership" we are talking about the process of dynamic cocreation in which leaders and followers are shaped.

For this reason, the popular understanding of leading through conflict offered by certain versions of family systems theories of groups must be significantly expanded and deepened.[8] Family systems theory helpfully claims that the ability of the leader to be self-differentiated within the group is an important part of effective leading. However, family systems theory does not fully account for the dynamically irrational forces of group life that push and pull leaders and followers alike in powerful ways that must be appreciated, known, and accepted in grace. As will become clear later, it is only in being able to accept and respond to that reality that the congregation will have any chance at all of actually learning from its experience in ways that might enable it to participate more deeply in God's transforming presence. Another, perhaps more provocative, way to say this is that it is unrealistic for leaders who allow themselves to actually know the irrational, unconscious concerns of a group to remain nonanxious. Although it is helpful to reduce anxiety if a group is to think clearly through its decisions to move forward, there are multiple gifts within the group that can help reduce this anxiety other than just the self-determination of the designated leader to be "nonanxious." The paradox is that for the designated leader to be nonanxious, the authorization of the group is required. Leadership and followership in situations of conflict, as we will show, are dynamically recursive processes in group life; in other words, they ongoingly shape each other.

Therefore, this book is not offering preconceived notions of how leaders are to lead in conflict. It is not primarily about developing sets of skills that can be applied in whatever context might arise. We will offer some advice about skills, but only in the context of deepening our understanding of the group dynamics of congregations so that leaders and followers might help the church be a space for God's transforming power for new life. Congregations must create leadership (that is, must cocreate leaders and followers) who can help manage the natural vitality of conflict for the sake of discovering the "new thing that God is doing." It is not something that people can know ahead of time, but it is discovered as a given community of people within a given context of history and with certain resources works together to follow the unseen God into the unknown future.

Finally, it is important to note that understandings of congregational leadership are shaped by and, in turn, shape understandings of God. The dynamic cocreation that happens within and between groups also happens between God and the world. God's presence in congregations, therefore, occurs in the messy, chaotic flux of the ongoing meeting of God and persons. God's desire for a congregation is discovered only by a restless, creative dialogue among its members and with God regarding its context, its historical theology, and its unique gifts and resources. Only a congregation that is fully engaged in this type of dialogue can discover God's desire for itself. Decisions for actions will be taken and tested within its current context. Mistakes will be made. We will not always get it right. Sometimes it is only by getting it wrong (sometimes dramatically so) that we can come to know better what might be creatively possible. We can only know the consequence of the strategies we develop after we have acted. Leading congregations in conflict, then, is trying, failing, forgiving, and learning from our efforts and allowing those to shape our next efforts. In the midst of our understanding and misunderstanding, our effective and our ineffective actions, our strengths and our limits, we live together in community and experience grace and mercy, joy and sorrow, accomplishment of love and disappointment. We experience the presence of the God who loves the diverse and chaotic experience we call life.

Some Important Things about Conflict

Of course, leadership isn't the only thing this book re-visions. It also thinks in a different way about conflict. It is important here to discuss some of the dimensions of conflict on which later discussions will draw. Conflict is not easy to define. The definition of *conflict* is itself conflicted terrain among those who study it. Rather than go over all the various possibilities, we are simply going to state what we will mean by *conflict* in this book: conflict emerges when we experience some kind of incompatibility among interests, projects, beliefs, or needs.[9] There is, in other words, a lack of fit, a sense that two or more people, ideas, feelings, or things do not go together well. There is a sense of incongruity, a clash, or a contradiction. In addition, as Joseph Folger and his colleagues note, conflict usually entails some sense that this incompatibility is likely to produce interference with or hindrance to our ability to pursue what we value or desire. This incompatibility is felt and

8

thought to get in the way of or subvert things that are important to us.

Several other features of conflict also need to be noticed in order to understand more fully its relationship to the dynamics of leadership in groups. Four things about conflict are particularly important to observe because they will recur throughout this book. First, although it may seem obvious, it is important to notice who is in conflict. Conflict can be in me, between you and me, between us, or between them and us. Conflict can occur simply within us as individual persons. For example, as individuals we often experience conflicting (incompatible) feelings or thoughts about something or someone. We feel or think both one way and another toward the same person or idea. This kind of incompatibility is called *intrapsychic* conflict. Conflict can also occur between us as individuals and someone else. We can get at crosshairs with a spouse, a friend, a colleague, or a fellow member of the church. This is called *interpersonal* conflict. Conflict can also be experienced between subgroups in the group to which we belong. For example, congregational conflict often involves subgroups of persons within the congregation who are at odds with one another. This kind of incompatibility is called *intragroup* conflict. Finally, we may experience conflict between groups. Different congregations, families, companies, or nations, for example, might be competing or disagreeing about something. This kind of incompatibility is called *intergroup* conflict.

Congregational conflict usually involves several of these forms of conflict occurring at once. As the case studies in the next chapter show, intrapsychic conflict is usually intertwined with interpersonal, intragroup, or intergroup conflicts of various kinds. It is sufficient for now to be aware that conflict occurs at multiple, interacting levels at the same time and is best approached with sensitivity to that complexity.

A second important thing to notice about conflict is that the way a conflict unfolds in a group will be profoundly affected by the capacities and abilities of people to deal with incompatibility and interference. Some of us can tolerate a great deal of interference with our desires and interests, while others of us really struggle when our desires or needs are interfered with by someone else or by our own limitations or contradictions. Congregations are obviously composed of people with widely varying capacities to tolerate incompatibility and interference. Of course, all of us will have differing abilities at different times. And with those differing abilities to tolerate these things will be differing in the ways we respond to them when they arise. Some will hide, and some will strike out. Some will cede without a fight, and some will try to negotiate; some will try to get their own way at all costs. How conflict unfolds in a group will be affected, therefore, by how the varying capacities to deal with interference and incompatibility, and the differing ways we respond in the face of those things, mutually interact and shape one another in the concrete realities of group life. Groups use these differing capacities and defenses of their members for conscious and unconscious purposes: channeling the conflict in various ways, sacrificing certain members for the benefit of others, and elevating some longings and fears while hiding or obscuring others.

Third, the capacities and abilities of individuals and groups to tolerate and deal productively with incompatibility and interference are not just individual psychological matters. They are profoundly shaped by larger social and cultural dynamics. The ways in which cultures and groups categorize the social world and structurally disperse and restrain power and authority have profound formative influences on the shape and character of conflict within a group. Social categories such as gender, race, ethnicity, age, class, sexual orientation, liberalism and conservativism are used in the social distribution of resources in ways that affect conflict.[10] Likewise, more general cultural and social forces and meanings have a tendency to shape the ways in which conflict appears in congregational life. This should not be surprising. Just as leaders and followers in individual groups cocreate one another, so differing groups within a particular context cocreate one another in a social environment. As this book will show, conflict within a group never is just about that group's own internal dynamics but also is about its place within a broader social-cultural field of contested meanings and alternative groups.

Finally, because conflict is about incompatibility and interference, it is fundamentally about what we do with loss.[11] Conflict raises issues, and thus emotions, of loss that is believed to already have happened, loss that is felt to be in the process of happening, and loss that is imagined, threatened, or anticipated to happen in the future. Of course, loss in this sense is a matter of perspective. What is thought to be a loss by one person is counted a gain by another. People can disagree about whether a loss has occurred or whether it is reasonable to imagine that a loss might occur. Some losses we recognize and perceive. Other losses (and their consequences) are only unconsciously felt and enacted. It is because loss is so central to conflict that grieving well as individuals and groups is indispensable to dealing with conflict.

Some Important Things about Loss and Grief

With all change comes loss. Some changes are by choice. When that is the case, we decide that we will give up something for something else. If we choose to have a child, we decide to gain the presence of a new life in our family and at the same time to lose certain ways of living that are possible in the absence of a child. When we make choices to change, we are generally deciding on the basis of an assumption that the blessing or gain is worth the cost or loss. There are also many losses and many gains that we don't anticipate. Life lived results in discoveries that no one could have foreseen. However, there are other changes that are not chosen or anticipated. If a partner dies from an accident, the cost or loss is so profoundly intense that it takes a long and agonizing struggle to come to see the gain or blessing in the loss. In either case, however, loss is a component of change. We believe that this tension between gain and loss is the source of much of the conflict that occurs within individuals, congregations, and other organizations.

For individuals or groups to continue to live and thrive beyond a loss resulting from change, we believe that they must grieve the loss. In Dan Moseley's book, *Lose, Love, Live: The Spiritual Guide to Loss and Change*, he defines grieving as "learning to live in the absence of something significant."[12] Most of our intense conflicts are the result of either the loss or perceived loss of something that is central to our self-identity or sense of well-being. As individuals, the fabric of our lives is woven out of memories and experiences, including those associated with work and love. When

11

people have labored and sacrificed a lifetime for jobs that have sustained them and given them a sense of purpose, it is a radical loss when their days are no longer woven with the thread of that purpose. At the loss of a job, a person must learn to live again in the absence of that significant, purpose-producing activity.

Groups also weave a sense of identity and well-being with the threads of their interactions and activities. The rituals of a church become a way in which persons who are part of the church know themselves. People might say: "We are people who come together and sing those old Gospel songs. When we sing them, we are connected to our parents and grandparents and to those who taught us about God. Singing those songs helps us feel grounded in our faith and connects us to God." If a person comes into that church and starts singing different songs, the group's sense of itself may feel lost. For the church to live beyond that loss, it must learn to live without a significant part of who it knows itself to be.

Much of what we lose in the midst of change, while it produces conflict in us, can be processed relatively easily. The advice that is sometimes given to "get over it" or "just move on" can be easily understood. If we think about it, we can determine that the loss produced by change is not really that important or that what comes from the change is worth the cost. Most of the changes that occur in our lives as a result of changed circumstances are *metabolized* and absorbed into the new way of doing things. If a church changes from one caterer to another, there may not be much of a crisis. But for a church that moves from potluck dinners during which loving cooks have been offering their culinary gifts for decades and people have been tasting and sharing the spices and recipes for hundreds of meals, the change to a caterer might create more conflict. The intensity of the conflict is often related to the significance of the well-being and identity of that which has been lost. Therefore leadership in conflict must tend, as Ronald Heifetz and his colleagues have noted, to the losses that are at stake and the ways people tend to defend themselves against those losses.[13]

The intensity of conflict is related to the complexity of the resulting losses as seen through the four kinds of conflict listed above: intrapsychic, intragroup, interpersonal, and intergroup. Changes in our lives produce losses in one or more of these areas.

For example, a mother may experience deep intrapsychic pain over the loss of her child who is going away to college. At the same time, she may be losing the way she relates within the church because she no longer has her child with her in the pew. She may also be losing a connection in the community because she is no longer involved with the PTA at the school. Because of her deep sense of loss and vulnerability, a conflict within the church might take on much more significance to her than it would have done a year earlier when she was not grieving her intrapsychic or intergroup losses.

One other feature of loss in Western culture seems to play an important role in the conflicts that erupt in churches. Persons often hope for a sense of belonging or the security of home that is impossible to achieve completely. Home is where the rituals and practices of life are engrained, creating a sense of safety and a place to rest. This deep sense of home is often central to the religious imagination.[14] Achieving this sense of home is especially difficult within the current context of what Zygmunt Bauman calls "liquid times." In his book *Liquid Modernity*, Bauman suggests that the times we live in are more fluid than solid.[15] He quotes Paul Valéry, who says:

> Interruptions, incoherence, surprise are the ordinary conditions of our life. They have even become real needs for many people, whose minds are no longer fed . . . by anything but sudden changes and constantly renewed stimuli . . . We can no longer bear anything that lasts. We no longer know how to make boredom bear fruit. . . . It is now the smaller, the lighter, the portable that signifies improvement and "progress." Traveling light, rather than holding on tightly to things deemed attractive for their reliability and solidity—that is, for their heavy weight, substantiality and unyielding power of resistance—is now the asset of power.[16]

He suggests that in the current social and cultural milieu, becoming too grounded in the present form of things inhibits one's freedom to adapt to new and changing circumstances. He notes that John D. Rockefeller

> might have wished to make his factories, railroads and oilrigs big and bulky and own them for a long, long time to come . . .

[whereas] Bill Gates feels no regret when parting with possessions in which he took pride yesterday; it is the mind-boggling speed of circulation, of recycling, aging, dumping and replacement which brings profit today—not durability and lasting reliability of the product.[17]

Congregations are places where people seek, in part, some stability, predictability, and pattern that can ground and center their lives. They long to connect with a God on whom they can count. The rituals and liturgies of the church can create a sense of home and give persons an identity as belonging not only to a contemporary community but also to a community with continuity with the past. Of course, congregations are also places, theologically speaking, where discontinuity and rupture have historically been, and thus should be expected to be, present. They appropriately can be places where creativity and the breaking in of a new thing are welcomed and encouraged. Yet we have discovered in our work in congregations that because distress and fear are intensified, given the liquid character of our era, congregational conflict frequently emerges and is sustained as congregations fight over false dichotomies, for example, the seemingly conflicting vision of the congregation as a place of either a deep sense of home or a deep sense of transformation. Therefore, the fluid world of contemporary reality creates a critical subtext to the problem of loss in congregational conflict in our time that we will address more fully later in this book.

As this book makes clear, intense conflict in congregations is directly related to the coalition of energies that are enfolded by the ungrieved losses of the individuals and groups. A suggested change to the way the church is going to function or live will raise emotions related to other losses that lie within the individual's unconscious memory and in the collective unconscious memory of a congregation. Because the conflict has restored the power of those ungrieved losses and they are at work within the effort of the community to make decisions about the future, we believe that a more focused effort in helping congregations grieve is necessary. While chapter 5 develops this idea more fully, let us consider a couple of important dimensions of this process.

First, in learning to live again in the absence of something or someone significant (that is, to grieve well), it is critical that people (individuals or groups) are encouraged and helped to remember and reexperience the losses that they have and are experiencing. This is often an uncomfortable process because there may be tears and rage. People may feel threatened by their own vulnerability and the vulnerability of others, and that threat evokes discomfort in them. Pastoral sensitivity and patience are critical gifts of the Spirit during these times. The reflections and expressions that are heard reveal the power of the loss, and if they can be exposed and named and reexperienced in a space of grace and mercy, that energy might be released as positive power for the future rather than as a knotty fist of resistance to change. Leadership that helps create stability and solidity within the organization creates a context in which vulnerability might be expressed without fear of the organization becoming unglued.

A second dimension for grieving loss is the power of mercy and forgiveness as energy that frees the individual and groups to imagine and embrace the new possibility for life. The biblical image of God is one who is merciful and forgiving. God expects and requires just and loving behavior of the chosen ones, but God shows mercy and grace when they fail to live this vision. Mercy is a key theological understanding that is critical to grieving loss and therefore to processing conflict. Forgiveness is not the ability to forget the past, but it is the gift of being freed from the power of the loss of the past as the defining power for the future. Living again in the absence of someone or something significant is possible if the often still-present pain of our loss no longer controls what is possible in the future.

Leading a community of faith into an unknown future will require the presence of people who can attend to the losses that people fear or will experience when they make changes. The conflict over whether to move from where we are to where we are going, what roads we take to get from here to there, what to leave behind and what to embrace—these and other conflicts will create resistances that will have to be addressed. By helping people grieve the losses that come, leaders will help the energy of embraced blessing be released for the sake of a new future.

Some Important Things about Ministry

Because we believe leadership is formed in conflict and that conflict is inevitable in the experiencing of the vitality of life, we believe that ministry within the church is essentially grounded in the ability to process conflict. While ministry is many things, we believe that an essential dimension of ministry involves guiding and participating in circles of conversation within the community of faith to process conflict that results from diversity and change for the purpose of creating more just and loving relationships. This leadership is exerted by focusing in three different areas. First, a minister is one who is both a participant in and a leader among people who gather to engage in circles of conversation. Some of those conversations are formal and are created by structures that give intentionality to the conversation, while others are informal and are the result of people having relationships with one another. Groups that are assigned certain tasks and responsibilities work to fulfill their tasks for the sake of the whole. A minister is one who transcends the boundaries that delineate the groups to help them work for the benefit of the whole. Chris Ernst and Donna Chrobot-Mason affirm this function of leadership in suggesting that "boundary spanning leadership is the ability to create direction, alignment, and commitment across boundaries in service of a higher vision or goal."[18]

A second focus of ministerial leadership is centered in the processing of conflict that is created by diversity and change. The rapid increase of change and transition in our culture and world has created a significant increase in the conflict that comes as churches try to navigate the boundaries between the traditions and values of faith and the community they have developed and nurtured, as well as the changes that empower and affect individuals and the groups that are part of the church. Our society's rapid increase in communication and access to information and innovation all function to keep people off balance. The ability to hold values and beliefs long enough that they can be developed into practices and rituals that define and sustain identity is under constant challenge. This change combined with increased diversity, reduced respect for hierarchal authority, and the sharing of authority results in new forms of conflict for which we are often dramatically unprepared. Creating balance between leadership and followership within the context of this liquid matrix is a challenge at best.

Third, the ability to process conflict well requires that a leader help the community stay on its task in the midst of the anxiety and stress that would be inclined to divert it. When anxiety rises within the church, people are sometimes tempted to change their purposes. A church that sees its purpose as serving the world through community outreach may discover that it is tempted to make its purpose about keeping conflict from happening within the church. If that becomes its purpose, it has lost its identity and has become a different group with a different DNA.[19]

Ministry is about guiding and participating in conversations that process conflict because the purpose of the church is to bless the world with more justice and love. This goal of the church has been God's agenda as it has been revealed in the Hebrew/Christian Scripture and tradition. It is not the purpose of the church to create the reign of God on earth; it is to help identify where God is at work revealing that realm that is already present but not yet fully manifest and then to join the Divine in that activity. The role of the ministry of the church is to be engaged in the community of faith in such a wholehearted way that glimpses of the realm of God that are emerging in the community can be noted and celebrated. And ministry is to be concerned with the larger community of humanity so as to identify and guide the church to be invested in the signs of the realm of God as they emerge in the world. This ability to engage and embrace the new life that God is growing in the world is enhanced by the minister's ability to identify with losses that the church and the world suffer when God's realm begins to become clear and to help people grieve those losses. Ministry is about helping people learn to live without that which has formed their identity so that they can embrace the new identity that God is developing within them.

Who We Are and How We Got Interested in This Topic

We are writing this book because our experience has led us to believe that the literature on conflict in congregations needs to be enriched with the insights of psychoanalytic understandings of group dynamics and theological reflections on loss and change. We have been deeply involved both as laypersons and as professionals in the church and believe that the well-being of congregations is important for the culture in which we live.

K. Brynolf "Bernie" Lyon has been a congregational consultant for fifteen years, having grown up as the son and grandson of ministers in mainline congregations mostly in the Midwest. Educated at the University of Chicago, he has been a seminary professor for thirty years and has a private practice in psychoanalytic psychotherapy. He is a white, fifty-something male who is ordained in the Christian Church (Disciples of Christ) and who has spent the past fifteen years exploring group dynamics and group psychotherapy.

Dan Moseley's professional trajectory has had similarities but has been grounded in leadership in congregational life. After graduating from Vanderbilt University Divinity School, he served three congregations in the South and Midwest. When a series of significant losses struck, he was called to be a professor of practical theology in a seminary. He has grown up in the Christian Church (Disciples of Christ) and has been formed by the complex spiritual and emotional powers of multiple congregations.

Bernie Lyon's growing interest in the issue of conflict and how it functions in congregations was intensified during a particularly painful time of personal and relational conflict in his life. Dan Moseley's exploration of the issues of conflict and its relationship to the inability to grieve the losses of our lives grew out of his experience as a pastor and a season of loss of significant family members. As colleagues whose offices were across the hall from each other at Christian Theological Seminary, we began having conversations about what we were teaching. It became clear that Bernie's interest in group dynamics and the loss that must be grieved in group work was related to Dan's exploration of loss as the source of conflict in congregational life. We began developing joint insight while at the same time teaching courses on conflict and reconciliation together.

As we worked together and became friends, we came to believe that congregations' fear of conflict and its consequences often cause them to "tamp down" exciting and vital parts of the lives of members and their corporate life as a group so that there is "peace." The church's difficulty in dealing with the intense and diverse emotions and passions of its members often results in the church's denying significant creative passions within the community—passions necessary for human flourishing. The challenge of leading in conflict, we believe, is how to value both intensity and harmony, both the chaotic and unpredictable energies that give human life vitality and the needs for order and boundaries that make life together safe and trustworthy. We believe that the ability to regulate the emotional and spiritual life in a congregation in richer and more complex ways is one of the outcomes of grieving well.

We also noticed that congregations in conflict have an extremely difficult time making good use of the resources of their faith in relation to their conflict. Indeed, even most books on congregational conflict are paper-thin in terms of their theological sensibility. There are good psychodynamic reasons for this, as we will show in later chapters. Nonetheless, it seemed clear to us that helping leaders think through the challenges and opportunities of leadership in conflict as a practical theological dilemma was a critical task. This book, therefore, does not offer a systematic theological understanding of conflict and reconciliation but a practical theological one—one that emerges from and in dialogue with the dynamics of leading in conflict itself.

Because of these experiences and beliefs, we wanted to write this book to help congregations and ministers gain insight into their uneasiness about conflict and how they might reenvision the church as a community of vitality. As we will develop later in this book, we believe that this can best happen when congregations become locations for helping people grieve the ungrieved losses of their lives. We believe that groups fail to deal well with conflicts when ungrieved losses disrupt the normal processes for dealing with differences between and within us. Learning how to think about and practice the faith in community in ways that help us tend to the concrete vulnerabilities of loss and blessing will enhance the possibility for congregations to live more hopefully through conflict. Although this may not seem like an obvious way to think about conflict at this point, the burden of this book is to

19

help you see the emotional and spiritual connections that lie below the surface of our individual and communal lives.

What Is Coming?

Chapter 2 will develop this understanding of leadership with three stories of congregations in conflict. These stories introduce pastors and lay leaders caught in complex and painful processes that pull them and their congregations into intensifying spirals of conflict. These stories draw from real congregations with whom the authors have consulted, but they are finally creative narrative reconstructions that are meant to present in a new way dynamics with which readers are familiar. These stories will serve both to illustrate points throughout the book and to evoke in the reader her or his own stories of leading in conflict. We invite readers to remain open to their own experience of conflict situations that may resonate with or differentiate from these stories.

Chapter 3 will then move into a fuller understanding of the psychological dynamics that are at work in congregational conflict, developing several significant ideas from psychoanalytic group psychology that we believe make more realistically complex and dense the ambiguous and often oversimplified realities of conflict situations. In particular, this chapter shows how the failure to grieve fuels and shapes these dynamic processes in significant ways. Leaders who understand more deeply the dynamics that operate within individuals and groups during conflicted situations will discover helpful resources from within themselves to lead and guide the congregation in its conflict.

Chapter 4 will show how our failure to attend to our own and our congregation's experience blinds us to the resources that might contribute to producing positive outcomes. The spiritual and emotional dilemma we will address is this: how can we as individuals and congregations stay open to learning from our experience in intense conflict situations? The congregation needs to create and protect a "space for feeling-full thought" within and among persons and between persons and God—a space where intense feelings can be held, reflected on, and metabolized in ways that are faithful to the Spirit moving in the congregation's midst.

Chapter 5 will move us into the way in which congregations can shape their practices so as to comprehend and understand the psychological dynamics of loss and change. It will reveal a process for helping communities learn from their experiences. It will show how vital ministry is about processing conflict and how congregations can create settings for grieving the losses that come with change so that they can discover the directions in which God is calling them for the future. By attending well to the grieving process and shaping the organization's work around that process, congregations can grow in both vision and hope and release the energy and vitality of living into God's new future.

Chapter 6 will bring together the insights shared in the preceding chapters to reflect on the way preaching and the practice of liturgy might embody the conflicts of the congregation and create a special holding space in which these conflicts can be processed. Preaching is a kind of leading that also creates a context for cocreating more generally a congregation's representation of the vitality for life that is available to persons when they grieve their losses well and open themselves to the God who comes in the changing, unknown future. The liturgical practices of a congregation are the ritualized holding spaces in which the congregation processes its faith. This chapter will explore how the structure of the liturgy gives form to the congregation's discovery of new life change and loss.

The journey into conflict is a complex and emotionally charged space for creation of life and vitality. It is exciting and thick with the pain, uncertainty, and unexpected joys of adventure. We move into this journey of discovery as we explore how leading might be created and authorized within groups to help them grieve their losses and open themselves to the new life that is possible.

CHAPTER 2

Failing to Find What We Didn't Know We Needed: Three Stories

O might those sighs and tears return again
Into my breast and eyes, which I have spent,
That I might in this holy discontent
Mourn with some fruit, as I have mourned in vain.
—*John Donne*

Conflict, as we said in the introduction, is a normal, expectable aspect of life and ministry. It is, in fact, of their very essence. Most conflicts in congregations, of course, are dealt with in a relatively straightforward way. The disagreements, irritants, or confusions that might escalate into something more chronic or disruptive are metabolized into the ongoing life and conversation of the congregation or are mostly successfully suppressed. Although such conflicts might leave emotional marks on the participants, they do not cause longer or more virulent disruptions within the community as a whole or to the individual parties to the conflict. In such situations either we have had what we needed ready at hand to make our way forward or we have not immediately known what we needed but found it along the way without much trouble. We were able to access the resources needed and to make good use of those resources to move ahead.

Yet sometimes the conflict becomes more challenging. Sometimes we can neither know nor find what we most need to move ahead fruitfully.[1] As we will show throughout this book, in such moments our ability as leaders to learn from our experience and the congregation's ability to learn from its experience are profoundly compromised.

We believe that the difficulty in finding what we do not yet know we need at such times is often, in its deepest dimensions, about loss. Following the works of Jaco Hamman, Gerald Arbuckle, and Howard Stein, but in an even more encompassing sense that we will make clear later, we believe that these conflicts take root at the intersection of perceived, actual, and threatened losses in our personal histories and the perceived, actual, and threatened losses in the experience of our congregations.[2] The conflict itself is, among other things, an attempt not to grieve these losses—to imagine that the losses are not real or do not really have to happen (or, at least, do not have to happen to us). The failure to grieve well is, from our perspective, a core spiritual, emotional, and group dynamic that must be confronted amid the difficult conflicts we face in our congregations. When conflict becomes entrenched in congregations, in other words, when the usual means of dealing with it are not working, when we cannot find what we most need to move us forward, we believe a primary cause may often be found in the enduring, painful residue of ungrieved loss as it becomes entangled with the dynamics of the congregation-as-a-whole.

We want to invite you into this way of thinking about congregational conflict by telling three stories. The first is a story told from the perspective of the relatively new pastor of a congregation who suddenly finds herself squarely in the midst of troubled relationships. The second involves the pastor of a large and growing urban congregation whose success evokes an unresolved, traumatic past. The third is a story told from the perspective of the chief lay leader in a congregation who is thrust between warring theological and interpersonal factions in her congregation. The purpose of these stories is to help you begin to locate the outlines of the position we will develop more fully as our text proceeds. For now, simply notice the losses that the stories unfold—losses that pastors experience and bring with them into their ministry, as

24

well as losses with which lay leaders and congregational members struggle to cope—and the ways in which these intersect with one another and create powerful emotional and spiritual conflicts within the congregations.

Joining First Community Church

Mary Walsh was the pastor of First Community Church in Parkview, a city of some eighty thousand people in the Midwest. Reverend Walsh had been called to the seven-hundred-member congregation from a successful ministry in a smaller church in a smaller town in a neighboring state. Barely two years into her ministry, the trouble that to that point had seemed to her but a minor disturbance erupted in several lay leaders calling for her resignation in the middle of an angry congregational meeting. Confused and fearful that her ministry might abruptly end, she sought help from the denominational judicatory official with oversight responsibility for her congregation's geographic area. After lengthy conversations with most of the parties involved, the judicatory official seemed just as uncertain over it all.

What went wrong? Reverend Walsh had assumed that the discontent she experienced among some congregational members was a normal part of the transition in pastoral leadership. Sure, her family was having some difficulty with the move, but nothing had seemed so intense to her, no one so hostile as to prepare her for calls for her resignation. What had she missed? she wondered. How could she not have seen this coming? Her shock and questioning turned to anger as she brooded over matters in the days following the congregational meeting. Angry verbal clashes in the parking lot with the lay leaders who had called for her resignation, specially called meetings of church members either supporting or opposing her leadership, and threats to withhold monetary pledges and to leave the congregation entirely came in swift progression. What had happened? indeed.

First Community Church is a mainline congregation. Its members are no more aggressive or hostile or mean-spirited than those in most other congregations. Reverend Walsh had a good pastoral leadership experience for several years at another congregation. Her emotional and spiritual repertoire was no more limited or expansive than that of most other pastors. Just by these accounts, the conflict should not have happened. Or, at least, it should have been resolved through the normal conflict-resolving processes and procedures that this congregation and pastor had employed over and again in other contexts in their histories. Yet it did not. In an effort to make sense of this, let us tell you a bit more of their stories: first Pastor Walsh's story and then that of the congregation itself.

Reverend Walsh was forty-one years old when she was called to First Community Church. She had been married to Ryan for some eighteen years. She and Ryan had two young girls, fourteen and ten years old. The Walshes had been living in the town where Ryan had grown up. His parents and one of his siblings still lived there. The call, which had been so excitedly received by Reverend Walsh, was greeted in a lukewarm fashion by Ryan and the children. He would be leaving his parents, his sister, the community in which he was raised, and the job he had enjoyed at his best friend's department store. The girls would be leaving their grandparents and the first friends of their young lives. Although the move also carried numerous losses for Reverend Walsh, the professional advancement and new challenges it created were powerful compensations. Her husband and children experienced the losses far more pointedly than she did. They had serious ambivalence about the move.

Indeed, the family's struggle with the move came out in particularly prominent ways within the new congregation. First, Ryan and the children did not accompany Reverend Walsh when she first moved. Even though she moved in the summer so that the children would not have to change schools in the middle of a school year, and even though there was no house to sell that might delay their move, the rest of the family delayed for two months before themselves moving to the new city. Reverend Walsh worried that Ryan especially was having trouble with the emotional transition, and she shared that worry with a few members of the new congregation. Second, for the denomination of which First Community Church is a part, it is common practice for the pastor and the pastor's family to officially join the church to which they have been called. One year into the new ministry, neither

Reverend Walsh nor her family had officially moved their membership to the new congregation. Some lay leaders of the congregation spoke with Reverend Walsh about this on two occasions, suggesting that others in the congregation were noticing this failure to join with the congregation and raising concerns. Reverend Walsh kept the letter transferring their membership in her office desk drawer for six additional months after this conversation. Still she did not join the church.

Why was Reverend Walsh so resistant even after she had the letter prepared? When asked about this, Reverend Walsh expressed concern for her family. She knew, she said, that they were having a difficult time with the move, and she did not want to do anything precipitous that might further aggravate their feelings about the matter. Surely, she said, good Christians could understand and be sympathetic with her desire to do what was best for her family. Yet the longer Reverend Walsh spoke about the situation, the more another feeling seemed to emerge. Not simply concern, but anger, was present. She was angry that people in the congregation were putting pressure on her and her family to join the church. And with her anger came a passive-aggressive desire to do as she pleased, apart from what others might want. So she stalled, her hesitation an expression of a desire to control things that she felt she could not control or influence directly.

We might be curious at this point why Reverend Walsh took this approach to dealing with the family and congregational challenges she faced. Not surprising, of course, a passive-aggressive stance was not new or unfamiliar to her. She had grown up in a family in which her father was emotionally, and often physically, absent and where her mother looked to her to perform adult responsibilities well before she was of an age at which this would have been appropriate. Her mother, like most mothers, had expectations and demands of her. Yet there was something unusual here. Her mother had especially strict and rigid ideas about who and how her daughter should be. As a child Reverend Walsh was often resentful and angry that her mother used her to fill in for the absent father and that she seemed to care so little for Reverend Walsh's feelings and desires. Her resentment found expression in her hiding from her mother, trying to avoid being seen, pretending that she was busy doing other things. So when Reverend

Walsh put the letter for the transfer of membership in her desk drawer, she was again hiding, hiding from those others who had expectations of her that she felt were unreasonable or who failed to be sufficiently appreciative of the difficulty of her situation. In the logic of emotional life, it all made sense: expecting not to be seen, she hid.

While there is much more to the Walsh family story, what we have said so far may be enough for our purposes in this chapter. Now it might be helpful to turn to the story of First Community Church in order to see how these two stories came to be on a collision course. Again, there is far more to the church's story than we will report here. We intend to help you see enough, however, to help you begin to notice the prominence of the themes of loss and grief and their role in the conflict.

First Community Church had been a vital presence in Parkview for eighty-six years. It looked back on a proud history of witness and service in the community. It had run a food pantry and a Mother's Day Out program. It had supported Boy Scout and Girl Scout troops. It had joined ecumenically with other congregations in offering relief to poorer and transient members of the community. It was a vigorous financial supporter of its denomination's social justice and missionary work. It was especially proud of its choir and its music program, offering special services and productions to the city through its many years. Standing between this history and the future it had imagined for itself, however, stood its present reality: it had become an aging and shrinking congregation.

First Community Church had tied its future to Reverend Walsh's ministry in the hopes that she could reinvigorate the church. Her young family was seen as an asset to the evangelism efforts that had floundered over the final years of the previous pastor's ministry. The congregation, like many mainline churches, was growing older and smaller, failing to attract young persons to replace those members who had died or who had moved. At the time of Reverend Walsh's calling, the congregation was half the size it had been some thirty years earlier, and its annual budget had been reduced twice in the past three years. Contributions to social justice and missionary work, in which they had taken such pride, were reduced. Even the beloved choir had been forced to cut back its programming. This contraction of both its membership and its financial resources led many in the congregation to fear that its thriving was at stake. While no one was really worried about the survival of the congregation, the anxiety was high: could they continue to be who they had always known themselves to be?

So when Reverend Walsh arrived but her family did not, concern was immediately in the air. The young family that was to serve as a welcoming presence to young and newer members of the community failed to materialize. And when it did arrive, it was with a great deal of hesitation and ambivalence. The congregation's enthusiasm for its future, they felt, was not shared by the pastor's family. The hoped-for future seemed to be slipping between their fingers. Rumors started to fly: the pastor to whom they had tied their future was a fraud; she was getting a divorce; she was a hostile person who cared only about herself; she was spiritually bankrupt. In the absence of data, people will fill in the blanks themselves. As the unhappiness mounted and Reverend Walsh increasingly hid from that unhappiness, there were larger and larger blank spaces for congregational members to fill in from the reservoir of meanings they brought with them to the congregation from their own life histories.

As I noted above from the pastor's perspective, one and a half years into Reverend Walsh's ministry, two church elders set an appointment to talk with their pastor about the concerns that various members of the congregation were having and to express their own concerns about her family's not transferring their membership to First Community Church. Both were struck by what they took to be Reverend Walsh's lack of interest. They experienced her as brushing them off, not taking seriously the growing uneasiness they were hearing about within the congregation. Was she experiencing some kind of personal family trouble? Did she really know how to handle this kind of situation? Was she as competent a pastor and person as they had thought when the church extended the call? While they were concerned by these questions, they also wanted to give their new pastor the benefit of the doubt. They did not want to appear unsupportive or to be seen as undermining the pastor in a difficult transition. Surely, they felt, just as did their pastor, this was just a minor problem that would soon fade as the real work of her ministry with First Community Church took shape.

While Reverend Walsh may have given the appearance of being nonchalant about it all, she was concerned. Perhaps she was not as concerned as she should have been, but she was at least aware that things were difficult and embarrassing. Her husband and children were still distressed by the move and resisted transferring their church membership from the congregation they had formerly attended, the church was in a more difficult financial circumstance than she had thought, and now it appeared to her that certain church members were out to get rid of her. Nonetheless, she typed the letter requesting to join First Community Church, hoping that she could convince her family in the near future. As she typed and imagined the difficult conversations ahead with her family, her anger at the congregation grew. She put the letter in an envelope and placed it in her desk drawer. Six months after typing the letter (and after a second meeting with the elders) she still had not turned it in. The congregation was now divided and at loggerheads. Two months later several prominent church members called for her resignation.

Living with Trauma

Pastor Al Marquis had been serving Urban Chapel for six years when the possibility of expanding the church building was first broached. As a prominent African American congregation in an inner-city neighborhood in a large Southern city, the growth of the congregation had been a sign of renewal and a matter of great pride. God had been doing wonderful things through Urban Chapel, Pastor Marquis frequently noted: an after-school program for mentoring young African American males and females was a great success, a marriage enrichment program was attracting large numbers of couples from the tough urban neighborhood surrounding the church, a job bank had been created, and the Sunday worship service was now attracting nine hundred persons, nearly triple its size when Pastor Marquis first came to the church. It was time to build, many in the congregation said—a time to march confidently into the future God was providing. But when the congregation started to develop plans for this project, serious conflicts began to erupt.

The conflict was roughly between congregational members who wanted to build a community center and simply rework the interior space of the current building for worship purposes and those who wanted to build a new sanctuary. The first group, supporting a community center, consisted mostly of longtime members of the church who lived in the neighborhood. The second group, supporting a new sanctuary, contained mostly new members of the church who drove to the congregation from other areas of the city. This latter group tended to be wealthier congregants who were attracted by the charismatic preaching of Pastor Marquis. While this group appreciated the work the congregation did in the neighborhood, it was concerned that further growth would require a more glorious sanctuary to attract others from wealthier parts of the city. The group supporting the community center felt personally affronted by this idea, claiming that the church was in danger of losing its soul in pursuit of money.

Squarely in the middle of this conflict was Pastor Marquis. Pastor Marquis was no stranger to the street crime, gangs, deteriorating shops and houses, and general urban brawl of the area. He had grown up five blocks from the church, the oldest of three children raised by a widowed mother. Indeed, his father had been shot and killed on these streets when Pastor Marquis was two years old. Pastor Marquis knew all too well the debilitating effects of the racism of urban American life, the sense of having been left behind by a society concerned with money that his family did not have and access to power that his own seemingly limited prospects as a child appeared to foreclose. His mother, however, had cared for her children with tenacity and vigor. She demanded that they work hard at school and work to earn money in after-school jobs that they were then required to save for their education. Pastor Marquis remembers his mother with great affection as a strict but fair woman who made possible a life beyond the streets on which he grew up. Somehow his brother and sister did not get the message, he would sometimes wistfully say. His brother died in gang violence on the same streets as had his father, and his sister, pregnant at seventeen, had struggled financially to survive ever since.

When the emerging conflict at Urban Chapel took shape, Pastor Marquis felt deeply torn. His commitment to the congregation's neighborhood was profoundly personal. He had a sense that he could, perhaps, redeem his past here: his lost father and brother, his mother's anguish and long labor, his sister's frustrations and despair. And yet he also knew within his bones his own struggle to be free of this place, to be rid of its shackles, to move on and not look back, to make a home with others from outside the territory that had threatened to imprison him as a child. Pastor Marquis had returned to the streets of his childhood in the hopes of making something better for others and himself, but he was painfully conflicted about how that might be best done. He understood in a particular way from his own history the virtues of recruiting wealthier, middle-class givers from outside the neighborhood to bring relief and a sense of possibility, and he knew the virtues of digging into the neighborhood itself and making the church's commitment to it even more visible.

The financial and membership growth of Urban Chapel was entirely unexpected. The congregation, which belonged to a traditionally African American denomination, had struggled for nearly twenty years before the arrival of Pastor Marquis. But although the congregation worried constantly about how it would pay its bills, its longtime members were proud of the fact that they had nonetheless served the community in many ways, not letting their financial distress stop their expressions of commitment to the neighborhood and its people. This struggle to be faithful in financially desperate times was an important spiritual and emotional theme for many members of Urban Chapel. It was a sign of faith, they said, that they looked beyond their own need to the needs of others. This was their witness, and God required no less. It was also the case that most of the longtime members were persons who either had chosen not to leave the neighborhood or could not do so given their own limited resources.

The newer members of Urban Chapel were middle-class persons from the wealthier, northern suburbs of the city. They drove some twenty miles or more because they were committed, they said, to the mission of the congregation and because the preaching of Pastor Marquis was especially compelling. His rhetorical skills drew them, many would say, and the work of the church kept them. Surely they should blend well with the longer-term members, they had originally thought. Yet the socioeconomic class differences and the fact that they did not live their daily lives in the neighborhood of the church created deep divisions. Many of the newer members, like Pastor Marquis himself, had found ways out of the grinding poverty of neighborhoods like the one surrounding Urban Chapel. They thought that hope resided in bringing in more people from outside, like themselves, who could provide an additional infusion of money to support the work of the church.

The stage was set for the conflict at the annual congregational meeting. Ben Jackson, longtime member of the church and head of the Planning Committee, reported that the committee had prayerfully decided to recommend beginning the joyous work of expanding the church facility. The question was simply whether they should build a community center to strengthen the congregation's mission in the neighborhood or should build a new sanctuary. While the conversation began civilly enough, it soon veered into more heated debate. By the time the formal meeting ended and the informal meetings began in the hallways of the church, tempers were flaring, and Pastor Marquis's telephone was ringing, with both sides attempting to recruit the pastoral support that they felt confident would end the argument.

Pastor Marquis struggled with the conflict: he wanted to be fair to both factions within the church and, frankly, to find some relief from the distress of the conflict within himself. He thought about turning the question back to the Planning Committee, but he also felt that his role within Urban Chapel required that he be assertive in leadership and make the final decision. Three Sundays after the congregational meeting, Pastor Marquis strode to the pulpit and delivered a sermon, "God's Call to Our Future." God had shown him the future, he said, the future God desired for them, and that future involved Urban Chapel building a new sanctuary to serve as a glorious witness to the work God was doing in the world and in their neighborhood. Far from resolving the conflict, however, Pastor Marquis's sermon poured gasoline on the burning flames. Many of the church members who had opposed the building of a sanctuary were angry with him. He had, as one e-mail put it, "sold out his soul and the soul of the church." Longtime members grumbled that their pastor had lost his way, and some began to threaten to leave.

Pastor Marquis was frankly astounded by people's reactions. He couldn't make sense of them. In the church tradition in which Urban Chapel participated, the authority of the pastor was, while not necessarily unquestionable, certainly much stronger than would be assumed in most white mainline congregations. Yet the anger of both sides was near boiling. This became visible in a confrontation with Franklin Tucker, one of the elders of the church and a thirty-year member of Urban Chapel, who had been calling members to request their signatures on a petition opposing the new sanctuary. As told by Tucker, Pastor Marquis complained that he was encouraging insubordination. "I am the pastor of this church," Pastor Marquis said, "the one whom God has anointed to lead His people out of this wilderness into the future He has ordained for us. Do not stand in God's way." Tucker, wagging his finger in the pastor's face, shouted, "Pastor, you have confused yourself with God. We should throw you out of this place, just as Jesus did with the money lenders." Offended that his word had not closed the book on the conflict and, more secretly, shamed that his pastoral presence had not been enough to resolve the matter outright, Pastor Marquis became increasingly aggressive and hostile in his exchanges with those he began to call "enemies of the church." Of course, those opposed to him became increasingly aggressive and hostile to him and those supporting him as well. The "joyous work of expanding the church facility" had become a battle of conflicting desires rooted in a deadly and rigid mixture of shame, pride, anger, and fear.

Old and New Faith

Barbara Cooper was reluctant to answer the phone that cold Sunday night in February. She could see on her caller ID that the call was from either Bill or Sharon Binkley, longtime movers and shakers of Faith Church. She groaned to herself, knowing that the Binkleys were likely to be complaining again about the pastor at Faith, Ernest Brown. Ernest, she had heard a thousand times from them already, was a poor preacher, a sad excuse for a human being, and a poor choice for their small church in Cassville. She did not want to answer the phone. After church that morning, she had spent the afternoon at the local nursing home visiting with her father, who suffered from Alzheimer's disease. Just before the phone rang, she was talking to her daughter about her daughter's marital difficulties. Emotionally spent, Barbara did not want to answer the phone, but she did. As the chief lay leader in the congregation, it was part of her job. With a deep sigh, she lifted the receiver and tried to put on a cheery disposition.

What she heard was exactly what she expected. Bill Binkley was entirely dissatisfied with their pastor, and he wanted Barbara to do something about it. The sermon that morning was lousy again; surely even she could see that, he said. How much longer did they have to put up with this? Didn't she remember former Pastor Joe's sermons? Didn't she remember how inspiring they were? How was a church like theirs in a dying city supposed to grow if they didn't have someone in the pulpit who knew what he was doing? Why had they hired so inexperienced a pastor to begin with? Did she really want to be responsible for the death of their church? Then came the bombshell: Bill said that he had met with "several" church members of like mind and were preparing a petition to fire their pastor. As usual, Bill Binkley was gruff, aggressive, and angry. He had bullied his way around the church and city for many years, and tonight was no exception. Barbara tried to listen attentively but finally cut him off by saying she would consult with the executive committee and think about what to do.

Pastor Joe was Joseph Entleman, who had been the minister at Faith Church for the thirty-one years prior to the arrival of Ernest Brown. He was a former pastor much-beloved by most in the congregation. His wife, Marilyn, was a less-beloved former pastor's wife who continued to attend Faith Church after her husband's retirement. He also attended occasionally when he was not serving interim ministries at neighboring churches. This, as almost everyone knew, was surely a setup for disaster. With Marilyn's regular attendance and Joe's sporadic attendance at the church, loyalties among members were divided, and power struggles were frequent. Barbara knew this was a bad arrangement but was unsure what to do about it. Pastor Joe said that both he and Marilyn had offered to leave the church on numerous occasions but had been assured by congregational members, including the Binkleys, that their offer to leave was unnecessary. While denominational officials had attempted to intervene, the mainline denomination of which Faith Church is a part does not give judicatory officials the authority to mandate a change in this kind of situation. Ernest Brown knew of the difficulty, but he was confident in the assurances he received from the search committee that the presence of the Entlemans would not be allowed to become a problem. Four years later, the problems were mounting—and not simply regarding the Entlemans.

Cassville had been in serious economic decline since almost the moment of Ernest Brown's arrival at Faith. It had been a thriving city supported largely by the presence of three significant automotive or automotive parts factories. With the decline of the automotive industry, however, the economic and job base of Cassville had been severely affected. Jobs were being lost at an increasing pace, people who could not find employment (and who were able) moved to other cities in search of employment, and crime and bankruptcy filings were both on the upswing. The "better days" of Pastor Joe's ministry were tied not simply to his ministerial abilities but also to the economic and emotional climate of Cassville, both of which had suffered serious setbacks in the years since Ernest Brown's arrival.

Barbara felt badly for Ernest. He reminded her of her father, a decent but relatively ineffectual man who was desperately needing her care. Ernest had made a later-life career change when he entered seminary in his mid-fifties. Barbara knew that although Ernest was not a very good preacher, he had a good heart and sufficient administrative abilities to be holding the church together in complicated economic times. She felt stuck in the situation, however. There did not appear to be any good way to go. She experienced the Binkleys and their allies as bullies. They had come to the church in the first year of Pastor Joe's ministry at Faith and had been loyal followers ever since. She wondered if this harsh assault on Ernest Brown was simply another way of being loyal to Pastor Joe. Yet she also thought that not all of the criticisms they were leveling at Pastor Brown were off target. Barbara talked with the executive committee of the church and decided that she would hold a meeting with the church elders and the Binkleys to consider whether there was some solution to the present conflict that would not involve the firing of Ernest

Brown. It was not even possible to conceive of a conclusion involving the "firing" of the Entlemans.

When Ernest got the call from Barbara that a meeting was to be held, he felt upset. Why wasn't he invited? Was his perspective irrelevant to the situation? Did they not care about his perspective? After all, this was his first church after seminary, and he had spent these four years trying to work in an extremely difficult situation. With the longtime, beloved former pastor and his wife still participating in the congregation, he found it almost impossible to bring about the changes in the congregation that he felt were necessary for the church to survive in Cassville. Any suggested change felt like criticism of Pastor Joe to many persons, and, with Marilyn sitting on many of the committees, the tension was palpable. He felt that he was not as ineffectual as he appeared at Faith Church—that he was "made" ineffectual by the congregation's failure to stand up to the Entlemans and their allies. So on the day of the meeting, Ernest sat in his office and wrote his letter of resignation.

As the people gathered for the meeting that Barbara and the executive committee called, there was a sense of lightness that defended against the tension underneath it. Jokes were made, comments about the weather were offered back and forth, and concerns about one another's health were expressed. At the most superficial level, like most churches, members of Faith did not like conflict and preferred to imagine it did not exist in their small, family-like congregation. They were perhaps annoyed at being forced to face the conflict among them. Yet the opening banter connected them with one another in a safe way even as it disclosed the wariness they felt about the meeting. The space was being prepared, in any event, for the conflict to follow.

Barbara called the meeting to order, discussed its purpose, and asked the Binkleys to share their concerns about the pastor. Bill Binkley spoke, saying that the problem concerned Pastor Brown's inexperience in ministry and his tendency simply to act out of his inexperience rather than seek advice and counsel from members of the church. Sharon Binkley and three of the elders supplied a number of examples. He had used church money, for example, to buy a computer for the church secretary before getting final approval for the expenditure from the appropriate committee. No one attributed bad motives to him in this, it was more that he didn't know the procedure and didn't ask. Likewise, he made decisions about the use of the church sanctuary by nonmembers without first checking on the already-established policy, a policy they had spent a great deal of time developing with Pastor Joe. While these stories unfolded, the two other elders, clearly in support of Pastor Brown, began to object about the meaning of the incidents but quickly retreated to silence before finishing the sentences they had begun. Their retreat was too late. Bill Binkley had noticed the possibility of disagreement and immediately stepped in to assert what he thought was the bottom line: "Of course, this isn't really the most important thing. What is most important is that we are not being spiritually fed. He just can't preach."

Barbara asked Bill what he meant when he said he did not feel spiritually fed by Pastor Brown's sermons. After a pause, he said, "Well, he doesn't tell me what I want to hear." The three elders who had helped supply the stories of the pastor's inexperience nodded in agreement. "And what do you want to hear?" Barbara asked. "He never preaches about hell or the devil," he responded with apparent disgust. Perhaps it was just a projection of Barbara's own uneasiness at this response, but it seemed to her that the three elders who had been supporting the Binkleys squirmed in their seats at this point. One of them quickly added, "He doesn't have much to say about sin." A male elder who had begun to object previously, now objected in full force. "Look," he said, "it isn't about hell or the devil or the pastor's sermons; it's about the fact that we are a theologically diverse congregation, and Pastor Brown is too liberal for some folks. That's why you want him fired, and some of us aren't happy about it." The other elder who had been supportive of the pastor chimed in: "I just don't think the conservatives are being Christian about it." The elders who were on the receiving end of this comment responded in kind.

For the next several minutes, the conversation became chaotic as the elders argued and tossed *ad hominum* comments at "them" like grenades on a battlefield. But after this explosion of angry and accusatory feelings, the conversation turned to their hopes for the future and what they felt was needed in a pastor to lead them into it. The tempo of the conversation slowed abruptly. There were long pauses, a silent searching for words, and then a sentence or two followed by even longer pauses. While they doubted that Pastor Brown might help them in this regard, they feared that they would not have the resources to hire a better minister, since they were a financially poor congregation in an economically devastated city. They feared that their financial situation would leave them forever stuck in the spiritual mire in which they found themselves. They so longed for the days of Pastor Joe. The brief eruption of angry emotion was now lost in the slow, anguished search for words amid a dense cloud of hopelessness.

A Look Ahead

Understanding the stories of Mary Walsh, Al Marquis, Barbara Cooper, Ernest Brown, and the congregations they serve requires that we see the multiple contexts that shape these situations: the various emotional and church-related roles the participants fill, the emotional roles they play in their families of origin that shape how they take or enact their congregational roles in the present, the congregational histories that have led to the conflicts, and the economic, social, cultural, and spiritual environments of the churches and their members. The contextual domains, as can be seen in these narratives, interweave one another. Severe congregational conflict cannot be accurately described "thinly." It must be "thickly" described and complexly understood. This is what the practical theologian Richard Osmer has called the "descriptive-empirical"[3] task in practical theology or what Don Browning has called simply "descriptive theology."[4] We will offer some ways to describe and understand conflict in just these ways in the following chapters. For now, however, we want to return to our claim that conflict arises from loss and the failure to grieve and to focus on the role of loss and grief in congregational conflict.

Of all the things happening in the lives of Faith Church, Urban Chapel, and First Community Church, why are we asking you especially to focus on loss and grief? Why do we think these issues are particularly important to understand congregational conflict? On the one hand, of course, the stories themselves reveal that these congregations were experiencing profound changes or losses of various kinds. These changes and losses became inter-woven with the changes and losses experienced by the pastors and congregational leaders both in the immediate situation itself and also from their personal lives and their pasts. One need only look at the little we have shared about these stories to see the losses and changes add up: losses in early life, in the current per-sonal and family lives of persons, in the cities in which the congre-gations are located, in church programming, in personal and community identity, in financial resources, and even (and most profoundly) in the loss of hope. We are not saying that these losses caused the conflicts at these churches. We are certainly not saying that such losses, which are part of the ever-present realities of our lives, inevitably lead to severe congregational conflict. We are say-ing simply that loss that remains ungrieved or insufficiently grieved creates a kind of emotional complexity and density that can be drawn toward and can even intensify a spiraling emotional storm. It is our impression in working with many congregations experiencing conflict over the past several years that this dynamic is not unusual. In fact, we think it is the central dynamic experi-enced by most congregations in the midst of conflictual situations. It is what often blocks us from learning from our experience as individuals and congregations what we most need to know in order to move ahead fruitfully.

On the other hand, in the ways we have come to understand how individuals and groups function, we think there are good reasons to imagine that the failure to grieve is a core feature of personal and group conflict. In particular, various psychoanalytic perspectives on individual and group life focus our attention on the ways in which loss that cannot be grieved creates tendencies in our relationships that distort and disrupt. Indeed, psychoana-lytic thought is particularly suited to help us in this regard because, as Peter Homans noted many years ago, psychoanalysis itself arose as a mourning of the loss of "traditional" culture at the turn of the nineteenth century.[5] In order to reveal something of the way psychoanalytic thought talks about these issues, we want to offer brief examples from three of the domains of loss we spoke about in the first chapter: intrapsychic life, interpersonal interac-tions, and the intragroup dynamics. Loss, grief, and the failure to grieve occur, as we noted, in all three domains and, in effect, recursively interact with one another.

Many psychoanalytic authors over the years have described the grieving process as central to human development. Grieving is not just something that happens in the face of a death or that occurs only in extreme circumstances in our lives. Rather, our emotional development is itself somehow centrally concerned with grieving well, with facing the large and small disappointments in our lives (in addition to actual traumas) in ways that do not deny their painful realities but rather allow us to work through pain in its depth. When we cannot grieve well (and all of us, in different ways, have this experience), fault lines develop within our personalities: weaknesses or tendencies that lead to emotional difficulties develop and are ready to be *recruited*, or brought into play, when emotionally intense situations arise later in our lives. Some of these weaknesses may simply be quirks or annoying features of our personalities that get specially activated in stressful situations. Other of these weaknesses may derive from chronic distortions and rigidity within our ways of relating to ourselves and with others whom we face throughout our lives. The psychoanalyst Martha Stark stated it most boldly in describing what she thought was the psychotherapy patients' central dilemma:

> My contention is that the . . . patient is, ultimately, someone who has not yet grieved, has not yet confronted certain intolerably painful realities [regarding the most important people in his past and present]. Instead he protects himself from the pain of knowing the truth about [them] by clinging to misperceptions of them; holding on to his defensive need not to know enables him not to feel his grief.[6]

While Stark is referring to psychotherapy patients in particular, a couple of illustrations may help you see the kind of thing she means in a broader context that relates to everyone in different degrees.

All of us must confront the limitations of our parents, the ways they failed to protect us or acknowledge us or grant us an appropriate sense of autonomy. Of course, some parents are more dramatically compromised in their parenting abilities than others. But all parents are human and cannot provide perfect shelter, affirmation, and autonomy to their children; therefore, all of us have areas in our lives where we tend to feel misunderstood or unsafe or insufficiently connected to others. Being able to grieve the limitations of our parents is an important part of the developmental process. Yet for various reasons, sometimes (or in some areas of our lives) we cannot. We cannot, as Stark says, allow ourselves to know the truth about our parents.[7] And so we act as if they were perfect (that is, we deny their limitations), or we act resentfully toward them as if they could have been perfect if they had only tried hard enough (that is, we deny the inevitability of limitations). In either case, we fail to grieve the real limitations of the real-life parents we have had. This failure to grieve leaves us with the fault lines we discussed above, fault lines that often keep us from finding what we already know and from finding a way toward what we do not yet know—and most need to know—in the midst of conflict.

On the other hand, we must also confront our own limitations as people. Just as our parents could not be perfect, so we cannot either. We cannot protect ourselves or meet all of our own needs or recruit others successfully to meet our needs. Being able to grieve our own limitations well is an equally important part of the developmental process. Yet here, too, the failure to grieve is a common misfortune. To greater or lesser degrees, we may deny the real limitations that we have, imagining that if there is fault it must surely lie outside of us. Or we may take a hypercritical stance toward ourselves, as if we could be perfect if only we would put enough work into it.

There are, of course, many other variations of these issues, but the two illustrations above may be enough to give you a basic sense of what we are after here: all of us bring with us into our adulthood the residue of unresolved, developmental grief. Some of us also carry with us more traumatic, ungrieved losses from early life. These losses might involve abuse, death of a parent, or oppression by systematic distortions of social power, for example. Whether the losses we and our congregations bring with us into our ministries together are traumatic or developmental (or both) in character, these areas of unresolved grief are precisely the vulnerable spaces in our lives that may become most entangled and confused in situations of intense conflict. Current losses or challenges (in our families, our congregations, our cities, and our cultures) evoke earlier losses, and those earlier losses, to the extent they have not been grieved well, distort our experience of the current loss or challenge. In diverse ways, the stories of Mary Walsh and Al Marquis point to the complex interconnections between insufficiently grieved losses in early life and the way they took the role of pastor in the midst of conflict. These developmental losses (losses occurring early in life) interconnected with losses of different kinds in these congregations and fueled situations that soon spiraled out of control.

Group life presents us with even more complex dilemmas in relation to grief and loss.[8] In groups we have many people interacting with one another who have differing kinds of insufficiently grieved losses in their lives. Much of interpersonal conflict (that is, conflict among individuals) is triggered by clashing intrapsychic conflicts (conflicts within individuals). This is often visible in couples experiencing marital difficulty. Each party sees the other in distorted ways depending on how each adapted to early life losses: for example, one is perhaps defending herself against the fear of abandonment by relentlessly pursuing her partner while the other defends himself against the same fear by withdrawing.[9] The failure to grieve early-life losses well often produces this same kind of conflict among persons in groups: individuals defend themselves against the emotional pain of their ungrieved losses in ways that conflict with one another, that do not allow them to see the real other interacting with them, and that produce a variety of other difficulties that we will discuss in the following chapter. The conflict between Barbara Cooper and Bill Binkley is an example of just such an interpersonal conflict. Anyone who has spent any time in congregations knows examples of this kind of conflict and the difficulties it produces in congregational life.

Group life, however, is not only composed of interpersonal conflict. There is also conflict within and among groups or subgroups that itself is the product of the failure to grieve. Indeed, a good bit of what appears to be interpersonal conflict is actually embedded within these larger conflicts among groups. Much of congregational conflict is precisely of this kind. Here groups or subgroups form not out of the vulnerability from the loss that is threatened or actual but from people joining together in common social-emotional defenses against those losses. Think for example about the situation at Urban Chapel and the way two subgroups formed in response to the opportunities of new growth (and, we would say, the losses those "opportunities" covered over). Or think about the situation in Cassville and the subgroups that formed in response to the pastor. When psychoanalyst and group theorist Wilfred Bion spoke about the development of "basic assumption behavior" in groups, he was referring to the ways in which group members join together out of a common concern, fear, or terror regarding some threatened or actual loss (abandonment, helplessness, shame, loss of control).[10] What, we might wonder, were the common terrors that threatened the subgroups in the case studies above? We will describe these group-as-a-whole phenomena more fully in the next chapter.

Spirituality and the Failure to Grieve

The failure to grieve well is not only an emotional dynamic but also a spiritual one. Severe congregational conflict, in other words, is not only rooted in psychological dynamics but also more deeply in spiritual distortions. First Community Church, Urban Chapel, and Faith Church were all dealing not simply with conflicted systemic dynamics but also with profound spiritual issues as well. The emotional and spiritual are inevitably interconnected. Later in this book we want to offer a way to characterize that interconnection in a way that may help begin to reframe the issue of leadership in conflict as embedded within the spiritual and emotional struggle to learn from experience.

For now, however, it is important to note that while we are suggesting that congregational conflict frequently derives from the failure to grieve, we are *not* saying that the content of the conflict is unimportant. Whether Urban Chapel builds a new sanctuary or a community center, whether Reverend Walsh and her family join First Community Church, and how Faith Church is to deal with the economic devastation of its city, its own declining numbers, and its theological diversity are crucial questions in the lives of these congregations. They are questions that should be discussed and prayed about in ways that help these congregations make good, faithful decisions about their resources and their futures. Yet the conversations that the congregations most needed to have became derailed or impossible to develop fruitfully because of conflicts that disrupted rather than facilitated what needed to happen—conflicts that we are suggesting became intensified and destructive by the failure to grieve well.

We mean the stories we have presented here to be more than mere foils for points we want to make or demonstrate. The struggles of Mary Walsh, Al Marquis, and Barbara Cooper are not just illustrations for a sermon. We hope, rather, that you can connect with or resonate to their experiences. We hope that you can make your own life available enough to your reading of their stories to be drawn into those moments in your experience when you, too, could not find what you needed to know; when, in fact, you didn't even know what you needed and did not have it magically revealed. This book is written for and out of those moments when in the midst of conflict we have failed to find what we didn't know we needed. We think that there are hints amid it all—hints of a way forward that our failure to grieve keeps us from being able to formulate well. There are hints embedded in the losses we have kept from view. To be open to the future in a new way, we must be able to learn from our experience in the present; and to learn from our experience in the present, we must reattend to those losses that compel us to repeat a past we have failed to grieve.

CHAPTER 3

Taking and Being Taken by a Role: Getting Askew and Getting Aright

A new heart I will give you, and a new spirit
I will put within you; and I will remove from your body
the heart of stone and give you a heart of flesh.
—Ezekiel 36:26

For those who have gone to the trouble to take up the yoke of Christ, finding themselves suddenly askew in relation to others in the community of faith is a remarkably unpleasant and disturbing experience. Askew is something we get but rarely want. It throws us out of joint, out of sorts, out of whack, and off-kilter; we become unbalanced, misaligned, and discombobulated. When we get askew, as we do in conflict, we get worried or angry or afraid. We get ashamed, guilt-ridden, fragmented, or despairing. Of course, askew is also the kind of thing that can lead us to feel focused, intense, and passionate. Getting askew is a complex experience that evokes many different kinds of feelings, thoughts, and actions. No doubt as individuals we may specialize in one or another of these responses when we are involved in conflict. We may, like raccoons frozen in the bright lights of oncoming traffic, have but one response available to us when our feelings get above a certain intensity. But within any complex group of people, conflict will breed a fair amount of diversity in terms of basic emotional and behavioral repertoires. Some people will hide, while

47

others will come at you; some will be forceful, and others will be quiet; some will bite down and hold on, while others will try to appease; some will recruit supporters, and some will feel lost and alone. Some will try to do your job for and better than you, and some will not do even their own job at all. Getting askew is a complex thing.

How much more complex it is when we are supposed to provide leadership amid it all! Just ask Mary Walsh, Al Marquis, Barbara Cooper, or Ernest Brown. Each was struggling from within his or her own particular role about how to provide leadership for a congregation in the midst of conflict. Their ability to do so became increasingly compromised as the intrapsychic, interpersonal, and intragroup dynamics intensified. Leading in difficult conflict situations is almost always a struggle at all of these levels with the unmetabolized shards of disappointment (our own and that of others), whether consciously and unconsciously remembered, anticipated, or enacted.

The purpose of this chapter is to explore some psychological and spiritual dynamics of conflict as they shape our effort to take our role or roles within congregational life. To lead in conflict is, in effect, to take our role in a way that facilitates the work the group needs to do. Yet in conflict situations the way we take our role, and the ways others in the congregation may be inviting us to take it, can be anything but helpful: acting out ungrieved losses from our and their pasts, trying not to grieve the losses we currently face, even helping others block or ignore the losses they must otherwise work through for a productive outcome.

Getting askew, as well as getting aright, happens, in other words, in the midst of our struggle to take our role well. As we will see in this and the chapter that follows, leading in conflict is through and through a journey in Christian spiritual life, rather than merely a problem of "conflict management" or "conflict mediation."

One way to see this spiritual dimension of conflict is through the concept of vocation. In various Christian traditions, roles are important theologically because they are connected with the idea of vocation: the belief that God calls us to certain stations or positions in the world and, from that place, to serve God's transform-

48

ing of the world. Certainly for Martin Luther, one's vocation did not refer simply to paid work but also to the roles in which we find ourselves in our lives or to which we are drawn in the future by the invitation of God.[1] We believe, however, that it is more precise to say that the role is not the vocation itself but rather the means of the vocation. The role is comprised of the embodied social positions that we occupy and through which we seek to serve God's purposes. Our vocation, on the other hand, is to be alive to, with, and for the world: to serve God's purposes, to delight in God's enjoyment of the world, to suffer with those whose suffering God mourns, to seek God's justice for all, and to extend the compassion of God to all. That is a very broad notion. Our vocation is particularized, made concrete and real in the world, through the roles and relationships we take up or find ourselves taken up by. Yet the idea of vocation sets a frame of meaning around our efforts to take our roles well. It puts our individual desires in the context of God's desires. It invites us to struggle with the way we take our role as an expression of God's desires and purposes. The role we are authorized to perform is freighted in this perspective with emotional, moral, and theological weight: a weight that may help in or hinder us from performing our roles well in conflict. To see how this is the case, it is best to begin by talking about the struggle to take our roles in general, since, as the means of vocation, they identify the ways we are situated within a conflict.

Hirschhorn on Taking a Role

About the same time Edwin Friedman and others were popularizing the application of family systems theory to congregations and organizations of various kinds, a less-noticed but similar development was happening in psychoanalytic thought. For a variety of reasons, those developments were far less utilized and developed within the religious community. We believe those developments are important to recover, lift up, and extend. Although the application of family systems theory has undoubtedly produced many important benefits to pastors and congregations, we believe the developments in the application of psychoanalytic thought to group life help us see some things in new or different ways that are especially important for learning how to lead in conflict.

In the mid-1980s, the organizational theorist Larry Hirschhorn developed an influential interpretation of the psychodynamic challenges of taking a role. The basic problem we must deal with in taking our roles, Hirschhorn said, is confronting a double-edged risk and vulnerability: on the one hand, the risk and vulnerability that comes from the real, actual work required by our role and, on the other hand, the risk and uncertainty that comes from the ways our personal histories have shaped and misshaped our ability to mobilize our aggression appropriately in the service of our role. The first has to do with the difficulties and challenges that the real world itself presents to the work we are about. The second has to do with the ways in which we get in our own way and are unable to mobilize and use the inner resources we need to perform our role well.

Drawing largely on classic Freudian and object relations theories, Hirschhorn conceived of this second problem as primarily about the fate of aggression in our emotional development. Sometimes, he notes, we are not able to turn our aggressive energies appropriately toward the real difficulties and challenges of our work. Instead, either we turn our aggression toward ourselves in self-punishment, guilt, and shame, or we turn it toward things and people in ways that distract us from the actual work we have. Following family systems theory, Hirschhorn argued that this misdirection of aggression happens when the anxiety within the system becomes unmanageable. In these situations people "turn away from work realities and create a surreal world in which threats can be met with fantasies of omnipotence, dependence, or defensive denial."[2]

Most work has real risk, uncertainty, and vulnerability associated with it. This is certainly true for the work of congregational life today. The rapid pace of social change, the challenges of secularity,[3] massive economic shifts, and both the threats and possibilities of globalization and diversity all make the challenges of leading congregations today extremely challenging. Of course, the sheer lack of clarity in congregations about what roles actually entail can be confusing in and of itself, adding to the difficulty of taking a role well. Not having an agreed-upon sense of what is expected in the role, we are often left to stumble around a mine-field of conflicting expectations. The greater the uncertainty about what taking the role entails, the greater the likelihood we will step out of the role entirely. Indeed, role confusion is a frequent con-tributor to the kinds of stepping out of roles that happen in pas-toral burnout. Being told that we should differentiate ourselves in the face of this confusion is good advice as far as it goes, but it only goes so far, as we will see.

In any event, the real risk of the work that we face in our roles attracts emotionally primitive energies from our personalities like iron filings to a magnet when the anxiety, fear, or confusion becomes more than we can manage. Like the pastors and lay lead-ers we saw in the previous chapter, anxiety may cause us to step out of role—in Hirschhorn's language, turning our energies away from the real work we face. We end up imagining, for example, that someone will magically protect us or that the current situa-tion isn't really real or that we can somehow omnipotently control what is happening if only we try hard enough and get enough compliance from others or if we can hide away and not be seen for long enough that the conflict will go away. Reverend Walsh, for example, knew that people were distressed by her failure to join First Community Church, but she managed to construct a fantasy world in which this distress had no real consequences or in which everything somehow magically worked out in the end.

Hirschhorn noted that the anxiety not only can lead the individ-ual to step out of role but also can propel the whole organization off task. The way this misstep happens, he argued, was not simply through "triangulation," as in family systems theory, but rather through the formation of a kind of "collective fantasy" in which the whole system starts to act as if its task is something other than it is. Hirschhorn called these system-wide distortions *social defenses*, since they were meant to protect the organization from the unbearable risk and vulnerability of its real work.[4] We will explore these social defenses later in this chapter when we discuss "group-as-a-whole" behavior. For now it is simply enough to note that social defenses emerge when the individuals and the group itself are finding it impossible to stay in role or to do the real work they are authorized to do.

The end result, as Hirschhorn notes, is "as people step out of role they also step away from one another."[5] Others in the group tend to be seen less as they actually are and more as either all good or all bad caricatures. The further we move from the realities of our actual role in the real world, the more the persons who are there with us become others onto whom we project our own unresolved conflicts. They become characters in the unresolved drama from our inner world. Thus, in stepping out of role, we experience people not as they are but as we seem to need them to be.[6] We view them as persons who are persecuting us or who are inept rescuers or who are victims just like us, rather than the more complex people who they are. At the same time, these others in the group often get drawn into acting in ways that invite or reinforce these projections. A vicious cycle occurs. As the conflict fails to resolve itself by normal means, the unconscious pull into a collective fantasy becomes ever more irresistible and powerful.

Hirschhorn's theory is more complex than we have suggested here, but we hope we have presented enough for you to see something of yourself and your congregation in those moments when the anxiety of not knowing what you needed to move ahead became increasingly burdensome. Our purpose in presenting this theory is not to recommend it in toto. It is framed in an earlier version of psychoanalytic thought that itself must be expanded and enriched to be most helpful to us. However, it does lay out a framework that we find very useful and on which we want to build. The rest of this chapter will expand and enrich Hirschhorn's basic approach. We begin by examining a key ingredient in taking one's role well in conflict.

Emotional Regulation and the Meaning Resources of the Congregation

Conflict often produces intense and conflicting emotions within and between persons. As we mentioned earlier, most of the time these conflicts are dealt with in relatively straightforward ways: the disputes about the worship service or the pastor's failure to visit someone in the hospital or theological disagreements between parishioners about whom God is going to save are often resolved by agreeing to disagree (*holding* difference), by getting rid of one of the conflicting positions or people (*eliminating* difference), or by finding some way to work through the conflict toward some new ground (*metabolizing* difference). When the difference cannot be held, eliminated, or metabolized, it often becomes polarized. The *meaning resources* at the group/member boundary (at the boundary between the individual and the congregation) are not sufficient to help the conflicted parties move beyond the conflict. In other words, the languages, practices, organizational structures, and relationships that constitute the community are not able to hold, eliminate, or metabolize the conflict. Polarization normally intensifies the emotional environment and leads to varying degrees of fracture within the psychological functions of the congregation.

Emotional polarization is an expression of an underlying deficit that can emerge in conflict situations: the inhibition or distortion of our ability to make sense of our own and others' experiences. This capacity to make sense—to understand and explore the mental states, intentions, longings, and fears of ourselves and others—is, as the psychoanalyst Peter Fonagy and his colleagues note, a core ingredient in our ability to regulate our emotions well. Fonagy calls this the capacity to *mentalize*: the ability to hold our own and the others' minds in mind.[7] The better we can mentalize, the better we can grasp our own and others' intentions and feelings, the more likely we can regulate our emotions effectively, and the less likely it is that they will get away from us and cause hurtful consequences to ourselves and others. While Hirschhorn does not use the language of mentalizing, it is clear in his later work that he believes that developing the capacity to mentalize is increasingly important in our time for leaders to take their roles well.[8]

Congregations are, of course, composed of people who vary widely in their capacity to mentalize. Some are quite good at it, but others have had life experiences that have deeply impoverished their ability to mentalize well. And, frankly, all of us can slide into states in which our ability to mentalize is not very good. Chronic or especially disruptive conflict is almost always marked by failures in mentalizing that, in turn, further the conflict and make its effective resolution ever less likely. In the discussion of the psychological dynamics of conflict that follows, we will be talking about how our capacity to mentalize is affected by those dynamics, how they distort, disrupt, and basically throw us askew. To begin, let's look at what we will call the core emotional functions of the congregation.

When Hirschhorn developed his theory of taking a role, he focused on the challenges of mobilizing aggression in the service of the role. It is clear, however, that things other than or in addition to aggression can influence taking a role. In particular we want to highlight the influence of cohesiveness or lack of cohesiveness of the self on one's ability to take a role. Indeed, in some versions of psychoanalytic thought, problems with aggression are ultimately rooted in lack of self-cohesion. Many years ago the psychoanalyst Heinz Kohut developed a theory called psychoanalytic self psychology.[9] It has been further developed since his death and constitutes a major school of thought within the psychoanalytic tradition. Several people have applied his theory to the life of faith and congregational life in particular.[10] We want to use this theory to help you understand one of the things that happens when polarization sets in (which is also one of the reasons such polarization happens). The self, from Kohut's perspective, maintains its cohesiveness and its ability to regulate its emotions usefully through four basic emotional functions that exist in important relationships in our lives: *mirroring, idealizing, kinship*, and *efficacy*. The self, in other words, is made healthy by the soothing provided by relationships with idealizable others (idealizing), by a sense of being recognized and accepted (mirroring), by a sense of belonging to or being identified with significant others (kinship), and by feeling invited to assert ourselves in appropriate and productive ways (efficacy).

From our perspective, congregations and pastors often provide these functions in people's lives, just as congregations and their members can play these roles for pastors. Although people will differ in terms of which functions are most important for them and how intensely or frequently they draw on their congregations or pastors for support in these ways, these emotional functions can be seen as dimensions of the psychological functioning of congregations and ministry. When the meaning resources of a congregation cannot contain, eliminate, or metabolize differences in a congregation, the emotional functioning of the congregation and ministry in people's lives can be disrupted. People may feel unrecognized, like they don't belong, unable to soothe themselves in distress, unappreciated, or disrespected. They may feel emotionally injured or wounded and, therefore, may react with some intensity to the wound they feel. As self psychology observes, these negative feelings often produce shame responses in people. Unable to evoke the emotional functioning they need from the congregation or their pastor, and caught in the feelings of shame that evokes, they may attack others, attack themselves (as in masochistic responses), withdraw, or avoid the entire situation. Often in conflicted situations, shame produces an emotional game of hot potato, with shaming responses being evoked toward one another in a cyclical fashion. Productively managing our feelings of shame is one of the most important tasks in learning how to deal with conflict differently. Those who have been involved in congregational conflicts certainly know how disturbing these responses can be.

Think again about the situation of Reverend Walsh and First Community Church. Why were certain members of the church so distressed that she and her family were having trouble joining fully with the church and its ministry? Certainly it would have been disappointing, but why was it so intensely disappointing? Perhaps we might speculate that some congregational members needed their pastor to recognize or mirror their own sense of themselves in this especially fragile time in the life of the congregation. Perhaps they even took her hesitancy as a criticism of them. Thus, not only did she seem not to recognize their joys and longings, but also she seemed unwilling to identify herself with them in an important way. Perhaps others in the congregation wanted someone they could idealize or look up to. Perhaps her hesitancy suddenly removed her in their eyes from the throne they so wanted her to occupy among them. In any case, the failure of the pastor to support the emotional functioning that these persons were looking for from First Community Church and its ministry could well have provoked some of the intense emotional responses Reverend Walsh came to confront.

Of course, we might say similar things about Reverend Walsh and the emotional functions she was hoping that First Community Church and its members would provide for her. In other words, it may well be that she too needed them to recognize her. She needed them to mirror her own longings and joys, her own sense of herself as a competent and successful pastor. When she sensed they were not appreciating the complexity of her situation, she started to feel unseen in the deep and important ways in which she wanted to be seen. Feeling emotionally hurt and injured (and probably ashamed that she was not coming across as the skilled pastor she wanted to be), she became angry and withdrawn, unable to take her role in a vigorous and productive way.

Kohut believed that all people need others to help them perform these functions throughout their lives. We never outgrow our need for others in these ways. Yet some clearly have more intense, primitively organized, and chronic needs in this regard than others have. Why is that? Self psychology argues that there is a developmental process involved whereby if development proceeds as it ought, we become capable of performing more of these functions for ourselves than we could previously. Infants, for example, have far more difficulty soothing themselves than does the average adult. Basically, self psychology says, we internalize the capacity for greater self-soothing as we mourn the nontraumatic failures of others to perform those functions for us. In other words, all parents will be unable to meet these emotional needs perfectly all the time. Parental failures that are not traumatic can be the occasion for internalizing these functions, developing the ability to perform some of these things for ourselves. In effect, grieving well the failures of our caregivers allows us to mature. The failure to grieve well means that we will continue to expect and demand that others meet these emotional needs for us in intense and chronic ways or, even if we handle them well most of the time, that we will be vulnerable to disruptions in our ability to regulate our emotions capably in certain situations. The failure to grieve the losses in these developmental transitions, in other words, will remain with us, compromising our responses to losses and conflicts that are yet to come. They compromise, in effect, our ability to take our roles well.

Self psychology helps us see how difficulties in taking our roles well are not simply the products of failures in the ability to mobilize aggression in the service of the role's task but also can emerge from a lack of cohesiveness of the self. When our self fragments (or expresses its ongoing fragmentation), our ability to take our role well collapses. And the fragmentation of the self derives, as we have seen, from the failure to grieve.

Modes of Generating Experience

As we suggested above, ruptures in the core emotional functions of the self produce intense feelings and reactive behaviors that move us to either step out of role entirely (that is, act as if our role is something other than it is) or distort the way we take the role. We want to further suggest, however, that such ruptures produce shifts at the level of the basic modes through which experience is generated. Knowing how to understand these shifts and what they mean can help us better grasp how to appreciate what is happening when conflict becomes especially challenging. It is also an avenue into appreciating the emotional density involved in taking a role, a density even more challenging than Hirschhorn seems to have appreciated.

The psychoanalyst Thomas Ogden, drawing on and further developing the work of Melanie Klein, argued that human experience is generated through three modes. He named them the *autistic-contiguous* mode, the *paranoid-schizoid* mode, and the *depressive* mode. The names of these modes might seem a bit complicated, but we hope to show you that they point to and conceptualize dimensions of experience that are actually fairly near to all of our own life experiences. We will suggest that when conflict becomes challenging, experience comes to be generated in more rigid and less complex ways.

It will first be important to understand what Ogden means by the idea of the modes themselves. What does he mean when he says these are "modes of generating experience"?[11] Ogden is trying to point to the deepest cognitive-emotional ways in which our experience appears to us, the basic structures that organize and give shape to the flow of events in our lives, the core patterns of giving valence and meaning to our experience. Each mode, in other words, brings different kinds of things to the foreground and supplies different sorts of emotional and cognitive meanings to those things. Our experience is, Ogden is saying, generated through one or another of these modes. Although Ogden believes that there is a general developmental pattern to the modes, most of us have (or at least need to have) all three modes available to us. Indeed, this is part of what distinguishes Ogden's perspective from Hirschhorn's. Ogden believes that each mode provides essential and complementary dimensions to our experience. Let us describe the three modes and then give some examples to help clarify what is at stake here.

The developmentally earliest mode of generating experience, Ogden argues, is the autistic-contiguous mode. When experience is being generated in the autistic-contiguous mode, the felt bodily sense of edges, boundaries, and surfaces is in the foreground of our experience. Meaning is embodied in the ways in which our bodies locate themselves in the space they occupy. The autistic-contiguous mode provides the sensory floor that holds us up, contains us inside our skin, and provides a secure bodily sense of continuity and cohesiveness. When we are especially distressed, for example, we may sit on the floor or in a special chair, rub our skin, feel our feet on the ground by going for a long walk, or participate in a religious ritual in which our bodies are secured by the ritual activity. Sometimes in stressful situations we need to find again the sensory floor that will hold us. If we want to know why such intense conflicts in congregations can sometimes be produced by seemingly simple changes in the church building or its décor, we need look no further than the importance of the autistic-contiguous mode. One might wonder, for example, if the dispute at Urban Chapel between members proposing the building of a community center and members wanting a new sanctuary was made additionally intense because of the deep changes that would occur in the embodied, felt sense of self in whatever new space was anticipated. However joyful one might be about the new space, it would also be a kind of disorientation at the autistic-contiguous dimension that might well produce less balanced responses to the different ideas about that space.

The second mode of generating experience is what Ogden (following Klein) calls the paranoid-schizoid mode. This is the mode Hirschhorn had in mind when he spoke about stepping out of role. One of the essential elements of the paranoid-schizoid mode is called *splitting*. Splitting is an emotional defense in which emotionally conflicting feelings are split apart and vested in two distinct persons or ideas. So, for example, in a conflict situation, some people will see themselves as good and others as bad. Or they might see themselves as bad and others as good. Whichever way the split goes, the point is that emotionally complex people or ideas cannot be tolerated as complex, so the complexity is split apart into two opposites—good or bad. In splitting, people become caricatures of themselves with only the good qualities or only the bad qualities being seen.

A second element of the paranoid-schizoid mode is what Ogden refers to as the "rewriting of history." In this mode of generating experience, history is not a linear phenomenon. Rather, history is constantly available for re-writing. Nothing has happened that can't be altered. In the paranoid-schizoid mode, history is always written from the perspective of the dominant affect of the moment. Thus, if I hate you today, I will tell the story of our relationship from its beginning from the perspective of that hate. For example, you may have fooled me into thinking you were a good person, but now I know; now I get it; now the truth about you has been revealed.

Third, because in the paranoid-schizoid mode I am no longer seeing you as a complex person and our relationship as part of a continuous history, I am, in effect, objectifying both you and me. I am no longer treating you as a subject, with the feelings and intentions you have, but rather as an object that I can manipulate for my own purposes and according to my own perception of you.

The fourth, and most important, element of the paranoid-schizoid mode is a subconscious means of emotional communication distinctive to this way of generating experience: *projective identification*. The basic process of projective identification goes like this: I project some unwanted quality or aspect of myself onto someone else. The other person comes to identify with that quality, that is, accept it as if it was in fact the truth about them. I then relate to (attack, malign, care for, and so on) that quality in the other person as if it does not exist in me. All of this happens unconsciously, of course. Neither I nor the person onto whom I project the quality is consciously engaged in this process. It simply happens below the level of our awareness. For example, if I do not like qualities in me that might suggest I am sometimes lazy, I might see someone else as lazy and attack that quality in him or her. The quality that is projected can be anything, as long as it is one that I am troubled by in myself—one that I find unbearable in me. As we will see later in this chapter, projective identification is a key dynamic in groups—a means by which we create *identified patients, scapegoats,* and even the sense of the group-as-a-whole that we relate to in positive and negative ways. For now, though, let's address the third mode of generating experience: the depressive mode.

In the depressive mode of generating experience, history and time is now linear. Actions have happened that we cannot simply escape from by rewriting events. We have hurt others, others have hurt us, and there is no way to escape the realities of all that hurt except to mourn what has occurred and do whatever reparation is necessary to restore what relationship can be repaired. Good and bad are no longer split apart. Rather, we recognize ourselves and others as complex persons having both good and bad qualities, hurtful and helpful intentions. Others are subjects in the full sense. They have feelings and desires, fears and hopes that are not reducible to our own. "Others," in the full sense, now exist and must be dealt with as such in our relationships. We also are in some sense "other" to ourselves, having an unconscious life that escapes our self-knowledge, for better and for ill.

As we mentioned above, Ogden believes that all of the modes provide useful dimensions to our lives. We do not leave earlier modes behind as we mature, but rather we add the later to the earlier. Each mode needs and complements the others. In Hirschhorn's view, the problem involved in stepping out of role happens because the paranoid-schizoid mode has become activated. In Ogden's view, we would say, the difficulty does not emerge from one or another particular mode or from the existence of multiple modes but rather occurs when we collapse into one of the modes to the exclusion of the others. In conflict, for example, the parties often collapse into the paranoid-schizoid mode, unable to access the awareness of their own complex motives or those of their "enemies," both of which might be available through the depressive mode. The world divides into "us" and "them," and "they" are usually bad, mean, unchristian, unspiritual, and dangerous, whereas "we" are good, spiritual, right-minded, and, though perhaps misunderstood, are certainly well intentioned. This was clearly happening, for example, in the situation at Faith Church in Cassville. When the executive committee meeting exploded in ill will, the world was divided into conservatives and liberals, them and us. "They" were unchristian, and "we" were innocent bystanders. When the paranoid-schizoid mode of generating experience becomes activated in this way, there is no sense that our understanding of the situation is one perspective among others. Our perspective is simply the truth.

The Group-as-a-Whole

We can see the importance of Ogden's perspective for the challenges of taking our roles in conflict situations even more clearly as we show its connection to the functioning of group dynamics. You will remember that Hirschhorn spoke about social defenses as expressions of the organization's difficulty in facing the real risk and vulnerability of its work. The anxiety that produces the social defenses is often the product, from our perspective, of the anxiety of facing the real and threatened losses at the individual/congregation boundary as the congregation pursues its mission. In developing this perspective, we will be drawing on the classic theory of Wilfred Bion and its extension more recently by Earl Hopper.[12]

Many years ago Bion noticed that in times of distress groups and subgroups within larger groups tend to develop more or less unified emotional defenses against that distress, thus blocking the capacities that the groups normally have to do common tasks. In other words, the actual, real purpose of the group is often difficult to do either because the task itself is complicated to understand and perform or because the world in which the task must be accomplished is complicated, making it hard to do the work of the group well. As Hirschhorn noted, of course, this is also the product of the vulnerabilities embedded within the personal histories of the group's individual members. In any event, during moments in which the difficulties around the work task produce significant distress, the group often defends itself against that distress in relatively unified ways. Bion called these group-wide (or subgroup-wide) defenses *basic assumption behavior*. In other words, the group was acting *as if* its task was something other than its actual work task. It was acting as if there were another basic assumption operative in the group about what it should be doing.[13]

Bion argued that there were three basic assumptions: *dependency, fight-flight,* and *pairing*. In the basic assumption of dependency, the group is acting as if its task is to find a leader on whom to be dependent. In other words, confronted with the uncertainty and difficulty of its actual work task, the group reverts to looking for someone who will lead it out of the distress it is currently experiencing, someone on whom it can be dependent. For example, congregational members who feel that their pastor is not protecting them sufficiently from the distress they may be experiencing in the congregation will sometimes go in search of someone else in the congregation to be their leader, someone to whom they can give their support and loyalty, on whom they can depend, and who will lead them out of the desert and into the promised land of emotional relief. As Earl Hopper has noted, this is a kind of group behavior that is developed within a paranoid-schizoid mode of generating experience.[14] A whole group or subgroup, in other words, is collapsed into the paranoid-schizoid mode and acts as if its task is to find that idealized person who can serve as its leader amid its current distress.

A second basic assumption, fight-flight, is also produced through a paranoid-schizoid mode of generating experience. In this case, however, the group or subgroup is not using idealizing defenses but rather is using maligning defenses. Here the group is acting as if its task is to find an enemy either to fight or from whom to flee. The group is dealing with the distress generated by its work task, in other words, by looking for an enemy rather than a leader on whom to be dependent. In fight-flight mode, the group is looking for a fight-flight leader (someone who will take the fight-flight leader role in the group) who either will lead the charge against the enemy or will develop a strategy for retreat. In conflict situations, this is perhaps the most common social defense. As we saw in the Cassville congregation in the last chapter, the congregation divided itself into warring sides, each protecting what it thought was right, each constructing the other as the enemy.

The third basic assumption that Bion observed is pairing. Pairing takes place when a group acts as if its task is to find two persons in whose relationship the group invests the possibility of something new and creative occurring. In the face of group-wide depression or despair, for example, the group may look for two persons (often a male and a female) whose relationship the group will unconsciously cultivate in order to produce hope—the birth of a new thing that can save the group from the mire in which it finds itself. As Hopper observed, pairing is most often a response when the group or subgroup has collapsed into the depressive mode of generating experience. For instance, when the group is trapped in despair of the harm it has caused or the injury it has inflicted on others, it will sometimes look for a new creation generated by members within the group to offer new life to itself.

A fourth basic assumption in group behavior has recently been proposed by Earl Hopper. Hopper calls it the basic assumption of *incohesion: aggregation/massification*. This unruly phrase points, we think, to an important phenomenon often seen in congregational conflict. It develops, Hopper says, when groups are traumatized. In other words, when a trauma (which is the product of one or more intense losses) occurs in the group, the group can be threatened by being overwhelmed with shame or helplessness. Faced with this intense distress, it can act in one of two ways. On the one hand, it can act as if its task is to join together in an undifferentiated way (massification). In this response, the group permits no exceptions; all must be one. On the other hand, group members may simply exist side by side in the group without real connection (aggregation). In either case, the group or subgroup is acting as if its purpose is to avoid real emotional connection with one another, to keep its members safe from any further impinging trauma. Although Hopper does not put it this way, we would argue that this trauma-based basic assumption in groups collapses the group into functioning at the autistic-contiguous level.

Although we have been talking so far largely about group-as-a-whole phenomena from Bion's perspective, two additional understandings of these large-scale dynamics should be noted. Family systems theory talks about how emotional distress or anxiety within a system gets channeled or directed in order to move the anxiety away from one part of the system to another part.[15] So, for example, the term *triangulation* refers to the effort to move the anxiety within an interpersonal exchange to a third person or thing, in other words, to get someone else to carry the anxiety that this relationship is evoking in me. For instance, if I am distressed by something the pastor of my church has done, I might tell the church secretary rather than the pastor about my distress in an unconscious effort to evoke distress within the secretary and, thereby, move my distress from me to her or him. From the perspective developed in this book, triangulation works largely through processes of what we referred to above as projective identification.

A second interpretation of group-as-a-whole phenomena derives from *relational dissociation* theory in psychoanalytic thought.[16] In relational dissociation theory, the self is constructed through the links that develop (and fail to develop) among various states of mind. For example, the me that I experience when I am feeling ashamed in the presence of a shaming parent needs to be linked to the me that I experience when I am feeling proud in the presence of a congratulating parent and the me that I experience when being soothed by a calming parent. When trauma happens (either dramatic, invasive losses or losses rooted in chronic lack of validation of aspects of ourselves), we cannot integrate certain aspects of ourselves. Trauma compromises the grieving process that would otherwise help us integrate those parts of the self most connected to those losses. In human life there is inevitably a certain multiplicity within the self that results.

All of us have more and less well-integrated states of mind. We bring to our present lives the history of well-integrated, poorly integrated, and nonintegrated parts of the self. In group life, the less well-integrated and nonintegrated parts are ready to be recruited into conflict situations. They make us vulnerable to interpersonal distress that cannot be well regulated or contained. These parts of our self then get acted out through processes called *enactments* and *mutual enactments*. A mutual enactment is an emotional process in which some dissociated aspects of one person evoke dissociated aspects of others. Dissociation is a means of dealing with some unbearable state, removing the emotional links that might otherwise tie it to other aspects of the self. Because the state is dissociated, it remains unthinkable, without words to help us understand or mentalize about it. It can only be acted out, not spoken or thought. A mutual enactment, therefore, is when some aspect of one person that cannot be spoken or thought evokes aspects of other people that likewise cannot be spoken or thought. What results is a mutual enactment, a confusing, often hurtful exchange in which none of the parties really understand what is happening. From our perspective, mutual enactments can create or contribute to group-as-a-whole phenomena such as scapegoating, which we will discuss below.[17]

Sometimes when a conflict occurs in a congregation, almost the entire congregation will be absorbed in one basic assumption or one dissociated state. At other times, different parts of the congregation will react out of different basic assumptions or dissociated states. For example, one subgroup might react in fight-flight mode, while another might move into massification, and perhaps even another might act out of dependency or pairing assumptions. As with the modes of generating experience, all of these forms of group-as-a-whole behavior are important to group life. Sometimes we need to fight or flee, sometimes we need to be able to move into a dependency position or protect ourselves from further trauma by binding together as a less differentiated group. The problem, from our perspective, arises not from the group moving into basic assumption behavior *per se*, but rather when the group or subgroup collapses into, or becomes frozen in, one particular way of being as a group.

All of the conflicts we described in chapter 2 clearly illustrate how subgroups within churches variously started acting "as if" the task was to find an enemy to attack, a leader on whom to be dependent, or a way to manage the effects of earlier and current traumas. When this happened, the groups became unable to take in any new or disconfirming information about what was happening, which, as we will clarify in the next chapter, means that they were unable to learn from their experience. Since people "already knew," not even God is awaited as the bringer of a new thing. The only new thing needed is for the "others" to get it right.

The group-wide emotional defenses we have been talking about here have, as Hirschhorn knew, a powerful affect on our ability to take our role appropriately and productively. In attempting to avoid the real and anticipated losses we face (or the consequences of those losses), the defenses invite us, when they become rigidly held (rigidified), away from our real roles and tasks into a collective fantasy in which the congregation as a whole unconsciously acts as if its task is something other than it really is. The failure to grieve, as it appears in congregational conflict, weaves together the unmourned developmental losses of the congregation's individual members with the ungrieved or threatened losses in the congregation's past and current life to create a potentially volatile mixture.

Scapegoats, (Un)Authorized Others, and the Social Unconscious

The theories of Kohut, Fonagy, Ogden, Bion, Hopper, and others that we have outlined above provide us with ways to make sense of the psychological challenges of taking a role well in the midst of conflict. They help us extend and deepen Hirschhorn's work. We want to further develop this discussion by showing how their perspectives help us understand a few common role dynamics in conflicted situations: boundary confusions and the emergence of identified patients, scapegoats, and heroes.

Conflict sometimes begins with, but almost always eventually involves, boundary violations: someone's toes get stepped on, a trust is violated, a committee or group performs some action or makes some decision that actually is (or is perceived to be) within the authority of someone else, someone does more than he should or less than she should. As you can see, a boundary violation is almost always a failure to take one's role appropriately or productively. We usually think of boundary violations as involving someone *crossing* a role boundary, someone doing something more than or other than he or she should. But from the perspective we are developing here, a boundary violation can also involve a failure to perform one's role fully, a stepping too far back from the boundary of the role we have in the congregation—not doing too much, but doing too little.[18] In the first case we are doing more than we are authorized to do (role authority overextension). In the second case we are not doing fully what we have been authorized to do (role authority inhibition). Since the boundary of the role we have in the congregation (whether pastor, member, committee chair, or other) specifies the connections we have with persons in other roles, either kind of boundary violation creates or intensifies a lack of stability or felt safety within the congregation.[19]

As can be seen from our discussion above in this chapter, the violation of a role boundary can derive from (1) the fragmentation that accompanies chronic or acute fracturing of core emotional functions, (2) the collapsing into one or another mode of generating experience, or (3) the *rigidification* of the group or subgroup within basic assumption behavior. Think, for example, about the situation at Faith Church. Several boundary violations are clearly present: Pastor Brown's failures to follow church policy, the bullying behavior of the Binkleys, and the participation of the former pastor, Joe, and his wife, Marilyn, in the ongoing life of the congregation. It is likely, from our perspective, that all of these situations were both a product of, and were fueled by, disruptions in the core emotional functions and the sense of depletion or entitlement that can follow. As it became increasingly clear that the tensions within the congregation were not going to be transcended easily, the core emotional sustenance people looked for from the congregation became less available. The sort-of retirement of the beloved former pastor, his and his wife's continuing participation in the church, and the new pastor's inexperience and naiveté all contributed to, and came recursively to amplify, the failure of the meaning resources of the church to hold the conflict well. Likewise, the two subgroups that were revealed at the called meeting evidence a fight-flight behavior. Each group was feeling attacked by the other group and was attacking "them" in return. Both groups had lost interest or curiosity in understanding the others in any depth and treated the opposing group with shaming caricatures. Boundary violations often emerge, in other words, at the intersection of personal and group fragmentation and rigidification.

Another common dynamic within congregational conflict is the identifying of two emotional roles: identified patients and scapegoats. These are, we think, overlapping processes, but they are useful to distinguish. They derive from a common group motivation: to isolate "the problem" in someone else. In the identified patient phenomenon, the group seeks to relieve itself of its distress by locating the problem in some individual or subgroup. The group answers the question of why things have gone wrong, why it is experiencing the distress, by pointing its collective fingers at someone. In family systems theory, from which the idea of the identified patient derives, a classic example is a couple that is in distress, identifying a child's trouble at school as the heart of the couple's problem. The child is the identified patient here, the one whom the couple uses to keep the real sources of their difficulty from view. For the Binkleys in Faith Church, Pastor Brown is the problem. Pastor Brown is identified as the one who has or carries the problem. If, the Binkleys say, Pastor Brown could be cured or fired, things would be better.

In scapegoating, an additional process is added: not only is someone identified as the problem, but also the problem that the other person is said to have is actually a disowned quality of those identifying the person as having the problem.[20] In other words, in scapegoating some quality or aspect that we cannot bear or tolerate as part of ourselves is projected onto someone else. That person is then made to carry the fault or sin that, in fact, belongs to the whole group. A scapegoat is someone whom the group or subgroup sacrifices in order to avoid having to take responsibility for its own behavior. The unbearable quality that we all share (the hatred, shame, ineptitude) is located in another, where we attack it and then seek to restore the rest of the community to its moral or spiritual purity. Scapegoating is a prime instance of the kind of paranoid-schizoid functioning that appears in fight-flight basic assumption behavior in a group. Looking for an enemy to attack or flee from, the group finds the enemy it needs by locating its own disturbing impulses or qualities in a person or subgroup and then by rallying the troops, as it were, to charge or retreat.

Of course, scapegoats are not always purely innocent victims. Part of what makes this group dynamic so difficult to deal with is that scapegoats oftentimes do, in fact, share the quality that is being projected into them. Pastor Brown, for example, was inexperienced; he did on occasion do inept things in the church. So when some church members accused him of not being a good pastor, they were not pulling the accusation out of thin air. There were, in fact, things that provided data for the accusation. What those doing the accusing failed to notice, however, was that the church as a whole was also feeling inept, not good enough, like a failure. Its loss of members, the economic decline of its town, and its failure to appropriately manage the situation with its former pastor all threatened its own sense of esteem. Rather than acknowledge this vulnerability and anxiety with the congregation itself, various members of the church located the problem solely in its new pastor: surely he was the source of the distress with which they were struggling.

Congregations, and groups of all kinds, authorize people to perform roles on their behalf. Some of these roles are directly task or work related: the roles of pastor, committee chair or committee member, choir director, and secretary are all examples. The boundary violations we talked about above are all instances of violations of task- or work-related roles. However, groups also authorize members or subgroups to perform certain emotional functions within the group. So-called oppositional members (including scapegoats) or members who are chronically "nice" are often authorized by the group or subgroup to help it avoid or channel its distress. Such members are seen only from the perspective of a particular narrow band of qualities they possess (their arrogance or hostility or niceness or peculiarity) rather than the fuller range of qualities that in fact they have. These members are then used (or authorized) in their role by a group that unconsciously wants them in that role. The point here is that groups authorize members to serve both work-related and emotional roles, so understanding the fuller dynamics of the group-as-a-whole requires that we see the ways members are situated within the emotional dynamics of the larger system.

There is an old line in group dynamics that goes like this: whatever it is that hits the fan will not be evenly distributed. We might also say: whatever it is that hits the fan will not be *randomly* distributed. The ways that work roles, emotional roles, and scapegoating processes develop in a group are almost always influenced by what Earl Hopper has called "the social unconscious."[21] In other words, group life is always influenced in one way or another by powerful social factors and processes in ways that are often outside of awareness. The influence of class, gender, age, sexual orientation, and race, for example, have a kind of invisible, but nonetheless powerful, influence on what happens in group life. Congregations in conflict often find themselves enacting or participating in larger social inequalities or social structures expressed through dynamics of power, authority, and dependency.[22] Think, for example, about the situations of Reverend Walsh and Pastor Marquis. In what ways might gender and race have influenced what was happening in these congregations? There can be little doubt that the ways these conflicts unfolded were influenced by those social realities. Part of what must be mourned to move ahead fruitfully is our failure prophetically to live the gospel in the face of the principalities and powers of our world, the ways we live in the "not yet" as well as the "already," and the ways our relationships are governed more by the principles of social exchange than by those of the covenantal reality of God's realm.

Mentalizing, Distortion, and Rigidity

The perspective we have been developing on the dynamics of congregational conflict rests on a central important idea: the more we can tolerate and entertain alternative perspectives to our own, as well as others' behavior and experience, the more likely we will be able to find a productive way ahead. The point is not that this will eliminate conflict in our lives. Conflict, as we have said, is inevitable. The point, rather, is that we are more likely to deal with conflict well the more we are tolerant and listen well. The more we can hold alternatives as live options in us, the more likely we are to thrive amid being askew. Listen to how the psychoanalyst Donnell Stern puts this issue:

> If we are to perceive what something or someone is like, we must experience the possibility of alternative. To take advantage of the potential meanings embodied in interactive experience is to be open to multiple interpretations of oneself and the other. . . . To absorb the potential meaning of interpersonal events is to be

curious, allow oneself, with a willingness that derives not from moral force but from desire, to imagine as freely as possible the ways of grasping and feeling one's own and the other's conduct and experience. Unfettered curiosity is an ideal, never actually created but worthy of our aspirations toward it.[23]

When we get askew, in other words, part of what is off-kilter is our ability to make sense of our own and others' experience. Our perspective becomes too narrow, distorted, and rigid. We must, in effect, grieve the loss of certainty in our ways of understanding ourselves and the world. This underlying idea is rooted, we believe, in an understanding of human experience, in the problem of hermeneutics or interpretation more generally, and finally in some basic theological ideas about what it means to be human.

We observed earlier the point made by Peter Fonagy and his colleagues that the capacity to mentalize well is essential to being able to regulate our emotional lives productively. In other words, our ability to make sense of experience on the basis of feelings, longings, wishes, and so on is part of what helps us feel and express our emotions in ways that help us rather than hinder us. Fonagy says that we can fail to mentalize well in three different ways: (1) we may not mentalize much at all (as when we are collapsed into the autistic-contiguous mode), (2) we may mentalize in an impoverished or distorted way (as when we are collapsed into the paranoid-schizoid or depressive modes), or (3) we may misuse mentalizing (as when we manipulate others on the basis of our understanding of their feelings and desires). When we are in conflict, the dynamics that occur can be precisely those of a kind that inhibit our capacity to mentalize well, and not being able to mentalize well can exacerbate and prolong the conflict situation. Failing to mentalize well leads us, in other words, to intensify the ways we are askew.

One of the implications of this for leadership amid conflict is that congregational leaders must work at the capacity of mentalizing well in stressful situations. Edwin Friedman used to say that pastors must maintain a nonanxious presence. We think that it is more precise to say that pastors must maintain a mentalizing stance, nonreactively listening for, exploring, and acting out an effort to understand their own mental states and those of the other

71

conflicted parties. Even though it was not what Friedman meant, many pastors reading his work have assumed that he was suggesting they should aim at achieving a state in which they experience no anxiety in difficult situations. Yet anxiety is a normal human response to stressful situations. The pastor in conflict should be anxious. Indeed, the failure to be anxious may well mean that the pastor isn't mentalizing well at all—might be blocking out this or that aspect of the situation so as not to make herself or himself anxious. If we have the expectation that as leaders we are to "be calm and courageous no matter what," then we are actually less likely to understand what is going on around us in critical moments.[24] Being able to down-regulate our own "hot" emotions, of course, can be essential to mentalizing well and being fully available in most situations.[25] Nonetheless, if we are not available to those moments when the only way to know what is happening is to enact it, we are likely not paying attention to the depths of what is going on. The issue, in other words, is not the anxiety per se but rather the way in which the anxiety is handled. The anxiety must be handled by the pastor in such a way that mentalizing is deepened rather than foreclosed.

It may seem ironic, but often the only way we can deeply know what is going on is through those moments when we fail to mentalize well, when rather than remaining curious or calm, we have acted in anger or shame or envy or fear. In allowing ourselves to experience the moment, allowing the group to inhabit us, to haunt us with its longings and desires, we come to know those things in deeper and more compelling ways. To use the language of relational dissociation theory, finding ourselves in a mutual enactment (an enacting of our own and others' ungrieved losses) is sometimes the only way for us to understand what is otherwise unconscious and presymbolic. Sometimes the way out of a conflict is the way into it as well, at least long enough for us to find what we need for a different way ahead. Finding ourselves taken by our roles is just as important as taking our roles: we find our self-differentiating capacities lost to us, and in losing them we might find both our and the congregation's need more fully and vulnerably available to us. For this momentary loss of self-differentiation not simply to degenerate into what family systems theory most wants to protect against (an emotionally reactive leader who simply exacerbates the emotional distress in the congregation) requires an ability and a courage to learn from our experience, a challenge we will explore more fully in the following chapter.

Vocation and Role

We often talk about vocation as if it were some romantic journey toward finding the deep joy of discovering one's call by God to a place of profound, finally unambiguous satisfaction. By this measure, of course, conflict is always failure in vocation. Almost any biblical character who struggled with God's call, however, would tell us something else entirely: that vocation is, at best, a bittersweet wrestling with God that only rarely ends in God's submission. Vocation is more the long, painful, and joyful journey toward more fully realizing the heart God has given us: a broken heart of flesh. The challenges of taking and being taken by a role point, therefore, toward a larger spiritual dilemma. They remind us that human flourishing depends upon recognizing, grieving, and negotiating the irreconcilable within and among us, charting whatever trade routes we can between the islands of experiencing that make up the archipelago of our selves, and tending to justice and compassion as best we can in the midst of the violence we do to one another in the process. They remind us that subordinating ourselves to a communal purpose must be held in tension with subordinating the communal purpose to our own ends. They remind us that the point of it all is larger than we are and that we are larger than any point we can discursively name.

Indeed, the psychodynamic tensions we have described above seem to emerge from a more disturbing truth about us. They emerge as expressions of a more radical dilemma: as the psychoanalytic vision of life in groups we have articulated above seems to imply, the deepest longings of our hearts cannot be fulfilled, nor can they be simply given up. We live (knowingly and unknowingly, consciously and unconsciously), forever negotiating the arc between the two sides of this existential reality. This negotiation is somewhere near what we take to be the core of the spiritual dilemma, for these two sides of reality point through us and beyond us to that mystery that surrounds our very existence. This spiritual dilemma is, we think, the emotional matrix for what John Caputo calls the passion for the impossible—the passion for God.[26] The psychodynamic challenges of taking and being taken by a role reflect the passion for this impossible/Divine even as they defend against it. The risk is too great, the vulnerability too raw. To meet God face to face, one does not survive. And so the role, rather than being a place of meeting and disclosure, becomes a place closed and alienating. Or, rather, it is both at the same time. The spiritual life, too, it appears, is both taken and received. Perhaps this is merely to restate the Augustinian dilemma. On the one hand, our hearts are restless until they find their rest in God. On the other hand, finding this God in whom our hearts might rest is impossible, since anything we comprehend as God isn't.[27] Vocation is troubled at its root.

In the midst of this spiritual dilemma, from the perspective of Christian faith, it is important to remind ourselves that we are not redeemed by the roles we take or the ways we take them. The roles we take are not our vocation. They are instrumental means to our vocation, but not the vocation itself. God alone is the author of our redemption, and this is a free, unmerited gift. Our reluctance to take or be taken by our roles, or our taking or being taken by them in skewed ways, often reflects, amongst other things, a doubt as to whether such grace is real—a conscious or unconscious belief that perhaps we ourselves must safeguard our final security by the more proximate protections and defenses that we engage in our roles. If our role *is* our vocation, it becomes easy to confuse God's demand with the work of the role. Christian faith invites us into a sensibility, however, in which we can vigorously take, and be taken by, our roles since the larger question, the question of our final security, has already been decided. Nonetheless, it can be unsettling to realize that God's grace does not erase the consequences of who we are or who we are becoming. Nor does it help us avoid the more penultimate risks and vulnerabilities we face.

This basic claim of Christian faith is important also as corrective to certain demands the social unconscious may press upon us: the notion that the roles of women or persons of color or persons of a certain sexual orientation or class, or even white men are *essentially* this or that. Our only essential identity, we are reminded in

74

faith, lies in the realm of identity established by the covenant with God, not in the social expectations that structure relationships in the world apart from it.[28] We will see this again in chapter 5.

Yet to take and be taken by a role is not optional for us. There is challenge and opportunity on both sides: to take a role well we must face the risks and vulnerabilities of the ungrieved losses from our own past as these are evoked in the present; to be taken by our roles productively, we must face the risks and vulnerabilities of the ungrieved losses of the congregations we serve. Facing conflict, we often act and pray as if there were some alternative to all this. Occasionally the conflict obliges us, and we escape with all of our pasts intact and unmourned: a bargain perhaps not with the devil but with a relief that only rarely lasts for long—a vocation delayed. That we will always only grieve in part is no excuse, but it is the expression of the reality that God's realm is already present among us, but not yet in its fullness. Of course, we can take and be taken by our roles in better and worse ways. To learn the difference is a dimension of the spiritual journey during which we come to know ourselves, each and all, in the midst of a holy regret and empowering compassion, confronted with the consequences of our selves, held lovingly by God.

CHAPTER 4

Failing to Grieve and the Spiritual Discipline of Learning from Experience

Life is the art of drawing without an eraser.
—attributed to John Gardner

The distinction noted at the end of the second chapter between the content of a conflict (the issue about which we are disagreeing) and the process of the conflict (the way we are disagreeing) may seem to imply a clearer division than is actually the case. After all, as most books on these topics suggest about chronic conflict, we need to know how to change the *way* in which we are in conflict, even if we can't necessarily agree about the conflicted issues themselves. Surely we can find a way to change the processes discussed in the last chapter in a way that might open up greater likelihood of living well with the conflicts we have.

There is a truth in this. However, just as we have come to know that theory and practice are always deeply interrelated, so content and process are intertwined as well.[1] Content does not become content *for us* apart from a process by which that content happens. Likewise, a process always has particular content that it shapes. In an even deeper sense, any particular process of engaging a conflict has embedded within it all kinds of implicit theories or "content," and it is this content that makes sense of our engaging in that

77

particular process in the way we are. The content within the process may be known to us or unknown to us, but it is always present. The last chapter showed how we come to have a wide variety of beliefs about what is happening in the midst of conflict. But these beliefs come about through the process of the conflict itself. So although content and process are distinguishable, they are not separable. In any actual event in our lives, they interweave each other.

This point can be a complex one to grasp. But at least in one very important sense, it is nonetheless crucial to try to grasp it: the *way* we must learn and express well the Christian faith in our lives (the process) must itself be understood as a dimension of the *meaning* (or the content) of that faith. And the content of the faith can itself only be most deeply grasped in light of the process through which it must be understood and made personally alive and real for us. It is the density of this delicate dialectical exchange that is so often ruptured in the midst of congregational conflicts of the kind we are discussing in this book. We can end up holding our perspective on the conflicted issue, our sense of what God wants to happen in our community, for example, so dearly that we lose track of the pain that is caused by the process in which we are engaged. Alternatively we can end up so focused on the process of our exchanges with one another that we lose track of the spiritual and theological point that underlies it all. In order to get at this issue, we want to step back for a few moments to the challenge of ministry more generally and what we will call the spirituality of learning from experience.

The Problem of Learning from Experience

Several years ago, in their book *The Teaching Minister*, our colleagues Clark Williamson and Ron Allen argued that "the *central* task of ministry is *teaching* the Christian faith."[2] Noting that everything done by pastors and congregations in fact teaches something (whether right or wrong, good or bad), Williamson and Allen sought to help mainline churches recover a deeper and more encompassing theological sensibility about their lives as communities of faith, and, more precisely, about the nature of leadership in such communities. Their argument made (and makes) exceedingly good sense.

In our focus on the undercurrent of irrationality in group life and on the struggles of congregations in conflict more generally, we have come to reflect on why such a seemingly straightforward task as teaching the faith should go so untended, get so undermined, and be, frankly, so disturbingly muddled in the actual practice of congregational life. How does it so often happen that when a congregation most needs the resources of the faith in sorting out its life, it is those resources that are least likely to be fruitfully available?

Part of the answer, as Williamson and Allen observe, is that without the resources having been taught in the first place, they cannot be available in the present. We cannot hold congregational members in the midst of conflict accountable for knowing the advice in Matthew 18 about how to deal with persons with whom they disagree if, in fact, the congregation and its leaders have not thought it important enough to help its members reflect on the passage and work on forming their lives in ways that reflect its central convictions. Although this is certainly one reason for the failure of the resources of the faith to be present, there is also another answer: there is, we think, an active resistance to—and avoidance of—the kind of teaching and learning that are done as expressions of Christian faith. It is this active, if unconscious, resistance that is the focus of our concern here. As we noted at the conclusion of the last chapter, we cannot deal with conflict well if we cannot learn from our experience.

Many years ago Bernie Lyon began attending A. K. Rice training conferences on group dynamics conducted in the Tavistock tradition. He began attending these conferences soon after having begun to be invited into troubled congregations—ostensibly to do something useful in those situations. Struck by the limitations of his usefulness (he was easily frustrated by what appeared to him as the insistent unreasonableness of some folks and the subtle and not-so-subtle emotional brutality that characterizes such situations), he decided to try to gain some additional skills in dealing with groups. Additional skills, at least he thought, couldn't hurt.

For those readers unfamiliar with the Tavistock educational experience, a word of clarification is in order.[3] The conference is described as a temporary learning institution in which the task of the membership (those admitted to attend the conference) is to study the behavior of the group as it unfolds in the here and now of its three to nine days of existence. It works something like this: members are organized into small groups of eight to ten persons, put in a room with a consultant, and told simply to begin the task of studying the group's behavior. Likewise, the membership meets as a whole (some forty to sixty persons) with two or three consultants in chairs placed in a spiral and is told, simply, "You may begin" (if, in fact, they are told anything). It may seem an odd situation: a group of persons (some of whom know one another but many of whom do not) are sitting in a room, given the task to study their behavior as a group as it unfolds. The consultants who are in the room with the group rarely address individual members, rarely answer questions put to them, and, for the most part, do not even look at anyone in particular, but rather simply provide comments on occasion regarding what they think is happening in the group.

As you might imagine, what results is often a chaotic field of intense feelings and fantasies: anger and rage at what is felt to be the withholding or incompetent or persecuting consultant; desperate longings for deeper connections with one another and with the consultants now imagined to be distant but hopefully loving parents; wishes for acceptance and fears of rejection; disappointment at the entire institutional structure for failing to sufficiently nurture or soothe or protect in the face of anxieties that are evoked; envy of the consultant's position and power or of other members in the group who are imagined to have special relationships with the consultant or with one another; and despair over whether things will ever manage to be different than they are. The group, in other words, has ostensibly gathered for the purpose of learning from its experience about the nature of group dynamics, yet it very quickly resists doing so by becoming indifferent to, rageful at, or helpless in the face of its task. It subsequently begins to act as if its task is something quite different than it is.

As dramatic as all this may seem, it nonetheless mirrors important aspects of the experience of pastors and congregants stuck in the midst of congregational conflict. How did we get here? Surely someone isn't doing his or her job (or doing it well enough). That person is the problem, not us. If the pastor (or the choir director, or the church secretary, or the chief lay leader in the church) was a better person or a better Christian or was just more competent, we wouldn't be in this situation. The church has, in other words, gathered ostensibly for the task of worshiping God and, instead, finds itself acting as if its task were really something quite different. As noted in the previous chapter when talking about the group-as-a-whole, it often starts acting as if its task were to find an enemy to defeat, to find someone who knows what is going on who can lead the group out of the desert or rally it to defeat those who would cause it grief, or to act as if it needs to protect itself from other congregational members by huddling together in subgroups.

We spoke about the dynamics that create such outcomes in detail in the previous chapter. We want to take a step back at this point and consider the question of what is going on from a different, more general angle. Some forty years ago, the British psychoanalyst Wilfred Bion, the originator of the so-called Tavistock method for the study of group behavior that we described above, observed that people do not merely dislike learning from experience; they *hate* it.[4] Hate may seem like an awfully strong notion here (particularly when used in relation to people as generally reasonable as we all imagine ourselves to be). Indeed, when we have talked about these ideas with colleagues, pastors, and students, some people almost inevitably say, "Well, that may be true for some folks, but *I* really *love* learning from experience." What people tend to mean when they say this is that they learn better by working with people than by working with books. We continue to believe, however, that Bion chose his word carefully. To show why this is the case, we need to make an important distinction.

Adaptive Learning and the One Who Knows

To borrow a distinction from Ronald Heifetz, learning from experience can refer to at least two kinds of things, depending on the learning situation itself.[5] On the one hand, we might simply need to learn technical or applicational skills. In other words, what we learn from experience in this way is technical know-how or ways to apply knowledge or methods that are already known to problems that are already well defined by prior practitioners or participants. Lots of things we learned in seminary were of this sort: we were taught by mentors of one kind or another how to construct a budget or plan a committee meeting or deliver a sermon.

On the other hand, we sometimes need to learn new ways of being, new ways of seeing ourselves and the world, new ways of acting in a fundamentally transformed environment. Heifetz calls this latter type *adaptive learning*. It is precisely this latter kind of learning that we have in mind in this book: knowledge that we, in the midst of conflict, cannot find within the technical skills that we already have for dealing with that conflict. This is the kind of learning from experience that we hate. For it is precisely in these kinds of situations, Bion observed, that we must allow ourselves to know those dimensions of our lives (those dimensions of our suffering, in the broadest sense) that we normally keep at bay with well-developed psychological and spiritual defenses. Adaptive learning requires a profound jostling of our settled ways of doing and seeing things, and such jostling, to the extent it is happening at any depth, is painful and difficult. The problem is not just that we don't have the skills we need but rather that we cannot even know what we need to know to find our way ahead.

Adaptive learning of this sort, as opposed to at least certain kinds of technical learning, is passionally self-involving: it involves the transformation of some of our deepest and most urgently felt longings, hopes, and fears, not just as individuals but also as groups. The dilemma we are referring to might be put this way: in order to learn from passionally self-involving experience in a group, people actually have to make their passionally self-involved experience available to their own self-awareness and available for understanding within the group. Learning from experience in group life means learning *with* one another in ways that we normally avoid.[6] The vulnerability and pain that this learning process produces is significant. Shame and guilt emerge, with respect to what we are experiencing, as well as fear that others will emotionally harm and injure us (or that we will emotionally harm and injure others) if we reveal what we are feeling and thinking to others and, in some cases, even to ourselves. These emotions tend to keep things at a stalemate. The real and imagined costs of appearing (and being) stupid or incompetent or unworthy, or hateful or uncaring are high. Likewise, the belief that we *should* know what to do when, in fact, we cannot know often leads to a prison of embarrassment. The fears that we will be abandoned, dismissed, disappointed, humiliated, or rendered powerless in some significant way, in other words, tends to undercut the possibility of learning from experience.[7] To put it another way, the teaching and learning experience is powerfully filtered through the inevitable anxieties that arise in the very teaching and learning situation itself.

The too-frequent result is that much of what we count as teaching and learning in such circumstances occurs at a considerable distance from the depth and complexity of what is going on in us. We hope, of course, that people will go off somewhere, reflect on things, and come back transformed, having thought hard about the matter in the meantime and having kept the teaching and learning situation itself from becoming too messy. Sometimes, of course, people oblige us. What people frequently learn in this experience, however, is how to use a language (the language of faith, for example) in a way that keeps them safely distant from themselves and others and, in effect, from the transformative power of the faith itself.

The anxieties of learning from experience tend to evoke what we referred to in the last chapter as paranoid-schizoid phenomena.[8] One feature of paranoid-schizoid phenomena that is especially relevant to the hatred of learning from experience is the belief that either oneself or someone else already knows how to be in the world, thus saving oneself from the pains and insults of learning from experience. If, for example, I can simply absorb what you as pastor or teacher believe—or what "the church" believes or what "the Bible" says (taken here in some naïve fashion)—then I am saved from the struggle of learning from experience. Alternatively, if I believe I already know, without your help, thank you very much, whatever you say can slide off my back, as it were. In either case, however, the anxieties of learning from experience lead to defending the self and the community from the transformative potential of that very learning experience.

The failure of curiosity, the derailing of the human motivation of interest and exploration, bespeaks a much larger dilemma in human life.[9] As the philosopher and psychoanalyst Jonathon Lear has compellingly argued, the closure of meaning, the effort to cage the emotional and spiritual threats to the self and keep us safely within the confines of the range of meanings we already know, characterizes the resistance to the otherness of human life (and, we might add, to the Other who comes to us in faith).[10] Postmodern theology ups the ante on this issue, showing us that curiosity, the *resistance* to the closure of meaning, is essential to Christian faith and, indeed, to the very nature of language itself. In other words, the importance of keeping open the search for meaning is not simply reflective of the emotional realities of our lives, not just a recognition that "unformulated experience" is part of the human condition necessary for learning from experience. Rather, the resistance to the closure of meaning within the already known, the openness of the hermeneutical moment, the teaching and learning moment itself, is part and parcel of the human situation, as well as being indicative of the meaning of God for human life.[11] Failing to recognize this resistance in group life is, we believe, one of the most significant ways in which we double-bind community leaders as well as followers—a means through which we enact our conflicted hope that our group leaders or other group members will both engage us in the struggle to learn from experience and, at the same time, save us from it.

However much we might wish it were otherwise, learning from experience is not some individualistic process, which is what some people mean when they use the phrase. The "data," if you will, that is required to learn from experience is contained not simply within ourselves but within the larger communities that shape us, including but not limited to us as individual members. While the process of learning from experience is not individualistic, neither can it be circumvented by simply handing the process over to someone or something else. Such defensive enclosures of meaning within the already-known, thus avoiding learning and openness to the other/Other, must be seen for what they are: as ways in which we ever remake the golden calf even as we seek to move beyond it. The dilemma, of course, is that in conflict situations, the pressure on us to make a golden calf for some group or subgroup can be intense indeed.

Love, Hate, Grief, and the Vulnerability of Learning from Experience

So why do we have such a hard time learning from experience in adaptive learning situations? One important reason, Heifetz and his colleagues argue, is that adaptive learning—learning from experience, as we are talking about it here—requires facing the losses that accompany learning.[12] Or, as Tim Harford has recently put it in his book *Adapt: Why Success Always Begins with Failure*, we must make peace with our losses if we are to learn from our experience.[13] Since the loss of something we care about is painful, we often resist accepting the reality or the meaning of the loss. Forestalling the grief in one way or another, we fail to grieve. Failing to grieve, we cannot learn from the experience and move ahead, and we are primed to become entangled in situations that evoke our dissociated pain. And when we are entangled in these painful situations and conflicts, we do not learn.

The challenge involved is even greater than this. As Freud knew long ago, the painful quality of accepting loss is not simply that we are losing something we want. Any real relationship with something we care about, Freud argued, is characterized by multiple, conflicting feelings.[11] One way to describe the issue is that we hate (and envy, are jealous of, are bored by, fear, and so on) what we also love. Loss is painful not just because we have to deal with the loss of something we straightforwardly want, but because it ruptures a complex, ambivalent emotional field of feelings, longings, and fears.

In nearly all of the fifty-plus congregations in which we have served as a consultant over the past several years, the problems involved in grieving have reflected some variation of this theme. Although we are drawn toward the hope of the renewal of our lives by God's grace in Christian community, for example, we also resist and fight against the losses and the vulnerability that our learning this ever-new way of life threatens in us. As deeply as we long to serve God well in positions of church leadership, we also hate some of what our actual practice of leadership may threaten to teach us about who we are or about the faith we may actually be living as opposed to professing. We truly want what we most deeply want, but we most assuredly are made uncomfortable by the losses that come with getting it and the vulnerability that it seems to require of us.

Think about the story of Mary Walsh from the first case study in chapter 2. Her passive-aggressive personality style protected her from facing certain painful, vulnerable aspects of her early life: losses in her earliest family relationships that she managed not to grieve by submerging her aggressive energies in a cloud of unknowing. In her adulthood, when she accepted the position at First Community Church, she became unable to deal directly with the challenges she was facing. As long as she needed to dissociate or repress the threats that she feared, she was unable to learn from her experience at the church. She could only continually enact the losses, not learn from them and move forward.

As Reverend Walsh painfully learned, efforts to manage vulnerability by denying the depths of its reality are finally wrong-headed. In Kristine Culp's words, our vulnerability is part and parcel of our created nature: "Vulnerability is part of being creatures who are interdependent with persons, living things, and the cosmos."[15] It cannot, as she notes, be "superseded," however much we wish it could be. Many of us in fact entertain some version of the fantasy of the learning lottery. The idea of the lottery is that since some people seem to have gotten what they want (or can do what they do) seemingly effortlessly, without the injuries of learning from experience, perhaps someday we will too. God, as the great learning-lottery executive in the sky, will surely see to it eventually. In the meantime, our task is simply to protect ourselves from the cost of living above our heads. Apart from the fact that the lottery, as an old joke has it, is a way society has of oppressing the statistically impaired, the fantasy itself discloses something of the depth of the wish we have to protect ourselves from the emotional complexities of learning.

The basic point we are making here, and as many others have compellingly shown, is an obvious one that we nonetheless frequently fail to notice: the learning experience is not only cognitively complex but *emotionally* complex as well.[16] Since, by definition, a learning situation involves uncertainty and unknowing on our part, it inevitably evokes some sense of frustration, disappointment, shame, guilt, and envy just as it can evoke feelings of satisfaction, pleasure, pride, and joy. This emotional (and spiritual) density of the learning situation is amplified both by the particular emotional and spiritual histories we bring with us as individuals and by the peculiarly thick emotional dynamics within the group-as-a-whole in which the learning is taking place. Remember, for example, the situation of Pastor Al Marquis at Urban Chapel. His emotional history, the racial and cultural history of the neighborhood of the congregation and the wider society, and the tensions within the congregation as a whole between the two conflicting subgroups all coalesced to make the congregation's learning from its experience extraordinarily difficult. The emotional density of these kinds of learning situations is, of course, only further compounded when the learning at stake involves, as it does in Christian faith, our very sense of who we are and who God is.

The anxiety of teaching and learning Christian faith within congregations is also powerfully influenced by the social, political, and cultural situations faced by congregations in our time. Recall in this regard the changing economic and social situation of aging members and a stymied economy at Faith Church in Cassville or the complex collection of sociological forces at stake at Urban Chapel. The increasing fluidity and shrinking of congregational membership in many denominations, the shifting of the volunteer pool on which congregations depend, budgetary difficulties, gender and racial schisms, changing neighborhoods, the larger numbers of second-career pastors who seek theological education with families and a wide range of mid-adulthood responsibilities and expectations, the disorienting changes brought about by the use of various technologies in congregational life, the changing sense of pastoral and ecclesial authority, and the cultural shift from "mainline" to "sideline" all work to intensify the already-present anxieties of learning from experience in these situations.[17] Teaching and learning Christian faith, therefore, must often take place in an environment that actually amplifies the already-present anxiety of the task. While such anxiety can be the occasion for creative transformation, facing its multiple layers and meanings will inevitably be disorienting. As the philosopher and theologian John Caputo puts it, "The truth will make you free, but it does so by turning your life upside down."[18]

Both because of the inherent emotional and spiritual anxieties involved and the ways these are intensified and made more obscurely complex by sociocultural factors, pastors and congregations frequently want each other and themselves to "already know." The problem, of course, is that in their lives together, congregations and their pastors are attempting to address a question whose answer is not exhausted by the history of answers they rightfully draw on for guidance: how are we to live Christian faith here in this place with one another? Only if this question is abstracted from the concreteness of the lived reality of the situation that congregations and pastors actually confront can the answer be thought to be "already known." When this fact is correctly understood, it is rarely a happy recognition. Indeed, we hate the losses threatened by the vulnerability that arises in those moments when it is clear we do not know, when we realize at some level of our being that we need our own selves and the selves of others to be fully present in the learning community of faith in a quite different and risk-filled way.

The situation often becomes complicated in a hurry, however, because there is almost always at least one person (either the pastor or someone else in the congregation) in those moments who is willing to be nominated to be the one who already knows, thereby relieving the group of its awareness of its vulnerability. Unfortunately, this relief is temporary, since the cost of "already knowing" is the escalation of the vulnerability of disappointment. The underlying point here, in any case, is that we engage the learning experience of Christian faith with one eye focused toward what we long for and one eye focused away from it. We can, of course, bemoan this cross-eyed posture all we want, but it is, we think, simply a part of what it is to be human that is compellingly understood within the ironic strands of Christian faith itself.

Learning and Forgiveness

If we are surprised that congregations and pastors regularly fail to learn from their experience with one another in difficult situations, we do not have a complex enough sense of sin and vulnerability. And if we do not have a complex enough notion of sin and

88

vulnerability, we have a too-thin sense of forgiveness and grace also. And that, finally, is the dilemma. Learning from experience is inherently a messy business. People will hurt themselves and others in the process. For congregations and pastors who are committed to being nice to one another as their ultimate value or who participate in the church in the hopes that it will be the one place in their lives protected from the affronts and pains of daily living, this is a hard pill to swallow. And, frankly, no one in their right mind in the church *will* swallow it, unless that person has reason to hope it will not be the final word about his or her life. Learning from experience requires, as the organizational analyst Larry Hirschhorn and others have observed, trustworthy communities that in the very concreteness of their lives together practice the complex arts of confession, reparation, and forgiveness.[19]

Practices of cheap or superficial confession, reparation, and forgiveness clearly will not do in this regard. Too often in congregational life we short-circuit the struggle within the spiritual and emotional depths of reparation and forgiveness in order to avoid the pain of the "creative journey of forgiveness."[20] Members of congregations sometimes say that they want to either "get along" or "forget" what has happened; they tend to want to restore the veneer of geniality wherein they imagine their safety resides or to remain encapsulated within the hurt, anger, and disappointment that they experience. In the first case, as Robert Schreiter has observed, we often end up trivializing and cheapening what has happened.[21] In the second case, we are stuck, paralyzed by a past to which we cling and that diminishes our own and others' lives. Although human practices of reparation and forgiveness will always be partial, they are, nonetheless, the pathways for opening up the possibility of ever-greater learning from experience the extraordinary challenges and joys of Christian life in Christian community.

The arts and disciplines of confession, reparation, and forgiveness are, if you will, a net beneath us—a net that both holds us amid the anxiety of the transformative power of faith-in-community and constitutes in itself an enacting of that very faith that can only be learned from experience. Learning the Christian faith, in other words, is both made possible by and exemplified in participating in practices of forgiving and being forgiven. You will no doubt notice that there is a certain circularity to this: the faith must already be practiced well in order to learn it well. This circularity, amplified by the natural human ambivalence of love and hate in communities whose practice of the faith is always partial and fragmentary in any case, often threatens to imprison us at the surface of our lives.

Indeed, learning from experience only makes final sense, we believe, in the midst of two realities received in faith. The first is the faith that beyond our own faltering efforts to learn from experience as individuals and as a community there is disclosed One who holds the promise and the pain of the adventure of learning from experience in compassion, hope, and invitation. It is because our lives are ultimately secured beyond themselves, beyond our own partial and ambiguous efforts, that our struggles toward learning from experience can be seen as meaningful expressions of Christian spiritual life—as a seeking beyond our longing to secure what, in fact, cannot be secured by us. To borrow a phrase from Edward Farley, God "comes forth" *as* God precisely as we know more deeply the movement from "the passions of idolatry" to "the passions of freedom"; that is, as our being redeemed is known by us as historical event.[22]

The second reality received in faith is the radically incarnational perspective that God in certain important respects is struggling to learn from God's experience with us as well. We are suggesting, in other words, that the God of Christian faith is best seen not as one who "already knows," not as one who stands above or beyond it all waiting to see if we are going to get it right. God has not planned it all out in advance, waiting for it all to unfold according to some pregiven plan that it is our task to discern and follow. In this respect God is more, as Alfred North Whitehead used to say, the "fellow sufferer who understands"[23] than the One who already knows. God must learn from God's experience just as surely as we must learn from our experience.

Some will say, of course, "What good is a God if God doesn't already know?" Our response is simple: a God who is struggling to learn from experience is one whose authority and power are rooted in love and compassion, one who invites us into the heartbreaking and sometimes beautiful journey of being alive to the complexities of what is. The God whom we worship and to whom we turn in our own conflict, then, is one who is joined with us in the very depths of the struggle to learn from our experience as a community. We believe that this perspective on God is relatively more consistent with the biblical witness itself than one that embraces an already-knowing God, and that it respects the suffering and conflicts of human life without subverting the meaningfulness of the challenges of the human struggle to learn from experience.

The painful truth in all this is that the vulnerability we hate is, at the same time, the means through which we love; however, much of our journey toward that end is visible to us now only as in a mirror darkly. Our vulnerability, Kristine Culp observes, is both the occasion of suffering and the occasion of glory.[24] In this sense, Erik Erikson was quite right many years ago to associate the foundational emotional struggle in human life (trust versus mistrust) with the problem of faith.[25] As theologian Serene Jones makes us aware, beneath the ever-fragile and partial net of the practices of forgiveness must be a community whose primary quality is its steadfastness: its willingness to be there with one another and God, helping hold in "wonder and mourning" what can only be held in part.[26]

The moral of the story is this: teaching the Christian faith is the kind of activity that we are apt to *say* we want when we are in a position to believe we will not have to take it personally or, perhaps even more difficult, when we are in a position to believe we can take it as straightforwardly supportive of what we think of as our better, albeit oppressed or overburdened, selves. This is not an argument opposed to our colleagues Clark Williamson and Ron Allen, for, happily, this is a perfectly fine time to teach it. The hope that we will not have to take it personally, or can take it as simply uplifting, is often needed to provide the occasion for the transformative work that awaits us, even as it provides a set of defenses for resisting it. Over the long haul, the spiritual and emotional work of teaching and learning Christian faith lies in that paradox. The yoke of Jesus is light, its burden easy. Now go, sell all that you have, and follow him.[27]

91

Leadership, Followership, and the Discipline of Learning from Experience

In the long, hot summer of 2011, the dysfunction of the U.S. political system was fully on display as Democrats and Republicans did battle to raise the national debt ceiling. People of differing political persuasions will have various opinions, of course, on who are the heroes and villains—who was "us" and who was "them." Apart from blaming this or that group of people, the situation was clearly a political and cultural conflict of the worst sort, the kind of intensely polarized, viciously argued stalemate that characterizes so much disagreement in our time. Many members of both parties "already knew" what should happen, convinced of their ideological rightness so thoroughly that coming to a decision that in fact reflected the diversity of the wider social landscape became increasingly less likely. This way of being in conflict is becoming more deeply embedded in our culture generally, including in congregational life. What does it mean to learn from experience as leaders in our time?

We are suggesting in this chapter that good leaders in conflict situations are not persons who already know. Rather, good leaders are persons who can grieve well and help others grieve well the losses involved in conflict so that learning from experience can happen fruitfully. This may seem like an obvious and straightforward proposition, but it is not. One way to get hold of the difficulty and the opportunity is to look at three issues: (1) the problem of bad news, (2) the problem of secondary failures, and (3) the challenge of working with others to cocreate an environment in which learning from experience is a central feature.

Joseph Nye Jr., former Dean of Harvard University's Kennedy School of Government, has recently observed that learning how to receive bad news well is one of the most important dimensions of learning from experience for organizational leaders.[28] Yet most of us are notoriously bad at it. We give others the impression (in subtle and not-so-subtle ways) that bad news is not welcome and, therefore, inhibit others from sharing with us the very information from which we actually most need to learn. We can accomplish this inhibition, for example, by giving the impression that we are too emotionally fragile to handle bad news or too nice to hurt with bad news or, in fact, by unflappably contending that we already know it. Others give the impression that if bad news does exist, it is surely someone else's fault. Rigidly defended against the feelings implying that they might have participated in some way in something having gone awry, they look for others to blame. Still others, although open to imagining that bad news exists and isn't simply someone else's fault, give the impression that they are simply too overburdened to hear it productively. Of course, at the other end of the spectrum are pastors who are Christian masochists who have a hard time sharing the pain and guilt of things going wrong with anyone else. If something has gone wrong, they believe they are surely the source of it. For pastors ever looking for a cross on which to be crucified, the bad news that needs to be heard is distorted by their own self-punishing experience. In all of these instances, the invitation to others to share bad news is inhibited or distorted, making it unlikely that any learning will come from the bad news we need to hear.

The challenge is this: we need to receive bad news well, not because it is bad or because it is always necessarily right, but because it almost always carries within it some expression of threatened losses that both the congregation and pastor need to learn from and metabolize. Think about the situation at Cassville. When the phone rang, Barbara didn't want to hear the bad news. She knew it was coming. She had heard it before. She dreaded answering the phone. She struggled to stay open to what she was hearing. Like Barbara, all of us need to try to stay open to bad news even if we think the news being shared with us is mistaken or really just a manipulative effort in disguise. What matters most is being open to learning what is there to be learned and responding in a way that makes it more likely that the relevant others involved can learn something useful as well.

Some may be saying, however, "You know, I could hear bad news better if the people delivering it were not so mean or hostile about the way they did it." Admittedly, learning how to present bad news well (that is, in a way that others are more, rather than less, likely to hear it) is an important task that many of us might learn how to do better. Congregations could certainly be places where we learn how to do that in more productive ways. And, of

93

course, there are persons (some people unfortunately call them antagonists) whose ungrieved losses in early life have given them powerful defenses that get expressed in chronically hostile and aggressive ways. Like it or not, this is part of the diversity of humanity with which we must deal in congregational life. Learning how to deal well in community with the destructive ways in which some people express the intransigent pain with which they are scarred is a complex task. Learning that drawing firm boundaries can be an act of care can be difficult for some of us. Nonetheless, it is clear that blaming or shaming others for our own inability to learn from experience is not a way ahead even if it is blaming or shaming those who are blaming or shaming us. This only repeats cycles of unproductive relating.

To keep the interpersonal and group environment open to learning from experience, we must find ways not only to respond well to bad news but also to respond productively on those occasions when we have failed to respond well in the first place. In other words, there is a kind of "secondary failure" that can result when we do not notice and take responsibility for our blaming, shaming, or shutting out others. The problem of secondary failure is that it leaves the person or group delivering the bad news with no place to put their feelings and feared losses. In other words, without an openness to hearing the bad news and without a commitment to work with the bearers of bad news on how to learn from it, people will generally find someplace else to take their distress. They will either recruit others into the conflict in ways we discussed in the previous chapter or bury the distress inside themselves. In either case, learning from experience is thwarted or distorted. If we can notice the effect of our failure, however, it is sometimes possible to reengage the learning process.

Think for example about the situation that developed between Pastor Marquis and the elder Franklin Tucker. With the elder recruiting members to sign the petition opposing the new sanctuary, Pastor Marquis responded in anger. His anger simply fueled the oppositional response of Tucker and his allies. In other words, he failed to respond to the bad news well when it was first delivered. What we have not yet told you about this story, though, is that Pastor Marquis eventually noticed that his anger had failed to take seriously the real concerns of those who were opposed to

94

the sanctuary. Eventually, he apologized to Franklin Tucker for his response, asked for his forgiveness, and invited him to work with him on the issues. Although this did not simply erase the ill will, it did make a new beginning possible.

Perhaps it is clear that the challenge does not simply devolve to the leader. What is required is not only a leader who can learn well from experience but also one who with others in the community can help cocreate a challenging, forgiving community in which learning from experience is itself a spiritual discipline. Leaders and followers, as we have noted, cocreate one another. Learning from experience well requires emotional and spiritual authorization within the community. The more the community resists grieving its losses in ways we discussed in detail in the previous chapter, the more it forecloses the possibility of the spiritual discipline of learning from experience. The less well a community can learn from its experience, the more unproductive, even destructive, will be the conflicts in which it engages. In the next chapters we will discuss ways in which a congregation can engage the grieving process, opening up its capacity to learn from its experience about the future to which God is calling it. We will suggest that this learning is fundamentally a product of living deeply the liturgical rhythms of a community's life.

A Methodological Note: What Are We Learning from When We Learn from Experience?

The point we are trying to make in this chapter is potentially problematic on any number of counts. One that needs special mention, however, is the problem of the meaning of *experience* itself. We cannot address all the issues at stake here, of course, but given the intensely disputed character of this issue in North European thought in recent decades, some comment is necessary. We can put the question this way: when we speak of "learning from experience," from what exactly are we learning? What is "experience" in this sense?

The difficulty comes from two directions.[29] On the one hand, there are those who claim that experience is the private side of living—that which no one who did not directly undergo the experience could fully understand or grasp. Some say, "Well, that's just my experience" as a way of saying that no one can reasonably disagree because no one else has access to the data. Or some may say, "Well, that's a part of women's experience" or "men's experience," or "African American experience" as a way to say a shared reality within a particular group is not fully accessible to those outside the group. In any case, it refers to something individualistic or subgroup-wide that is otherwise inaccessible, private, and irreducible.

On the other hand, many have argued in the past forty years that experience is not private at all but rather the product of much broader social and linguistic practices and forces. In other words, experience, as it appears to us in our lives, is not the private, irreducible phenomenon it appears to be but rather appears as a result of the broader social and linguistic forces that give it shape, that make it possible for it to "appear" at all.

Since the issues involved here are obviously much more complex than we need to address given the purposes of this chapter, it is perhaps sufficient to note that the "experience" we are intending in this book recognizes both of the above. That is, experience is both socially constituted and private. The experience from which we are trying to learn in congregational life is in fact powerfully shaped by the linguistic and social practices of the community and the wider public world, but that does not exhaust without remainder the nature of our experience. It is also "ours" in some meaningful, personal/individual sense. As the historian of ideas Martin Jay has put it, " 'Experience,' we might say, is at the nodal point of the intersection between public language and private subjectivity, between expressible commonalities and the ineffability of the individual interior."[30] To use the language we introduced in our first chapter, our experience is cocreated. We both are its author and are authored through it and by it. Indeed, the "double-barreled quality of experience," to borrow William James's phrase, is part of what makes learning from experience so complex, so challenging, shaped as it is by private, subjective forces and meanings as well as haunted by, and inhabited by, sociocultural meanings and dynamics.[31]

Back Where We Began

As we have observed, practical theological issues are inherently complex because process and content, theory and practice, and the private and public dimensions of experience interweave one another. There is no way outside or around this issue. In conflict, however, congregations frequently act as if there were ways around it. They look for a biblical passage or a fundamental claim of the faith, for example, that can be used as the axis around which to change the situation in which they find themselves. Or they look for a way to pray together or for a conflict mediation strategy that might solve the dilemma in which they find themselves. In other words, they look for something or someone who "already knows" to use as an Archimedean point to move their world. The problem, we are suggesting, is deeper and more complex than this. The problem is more how we open ourselves to lean into, or to enter or engage with the deepest movements of the situation in order to learn from our experience with one another as we together figure a way ahead. This itself is a spiritual task through and through. Learning from experience becomes the spiritual site through which congregations in conflict wrestle with themselves and God—the place where they can engage with the practices and understandings they bring with them to the struggle.[39] It is the place in which congregations find themselves lost and lose themselves in finding themselves again; where grieving what must not be grieved is the impossibility that must be broached.

CHAPTER 5

Shaping the Congregational Journey: Losing Your Way to New Life

The heart of the wise is in the house of mourning . . .
—Ecclesiastes 7:4

The challenge of congregational conflict, we have been suggesting, looks like this: congregational conflict is often rooted in ungrieved losses. Complex losses at multiple levels make it difficult for us to learn from experience well enough to take our roles in productive ways in the midst of conflict. This difficulty is compounded by the de-skilling of congregations in conflict, the loss of the faith resources that congregations most need in order to learn from experience. Grieving loss, therefore, is essential to the spiritual discipline of learning from experience and subsequently to dealing well with conflict.

We want to propose a way ahead that roots the ability to learn from experience and, subsequently, the practice of grieving well in the deep liturgical rhythm of the church. In the processes of gathering, listening, offering, and departing only to begin again there is, we believe, a profound wisdom to living amid conflict as an essential ingredient to life. Leading in conflict is liturgical leadership in the deepest and fullest sense.

In this chapter we will be discussing the spiritual and emotional space of the "sanctuary," both literally and metaphorically

99

understood, as the space where the work of the people seeks to re-member itself with the work of God. We will be talking about the sanctuary as container for the emotional and spiritual challenges of grieving well and learning from experience in ways that help congregations thrive amid the conflicts that mark their lives. The liturgical rhythm underlying both the organizational and the spiritual life provides the space in which leaders and followers take and are taken by their roles as together they grieve with God toward the new life toward which God creates.

The Sanctuary

For a community to develop the capacity to grieve its losses well in order to engage the spiritual discipline of learning from its experience fruitfully, it must have a spiritual and emotional "structure" in which those processes can occur. The community needs to be a "holding space," a container for the intense expressions of life in its midst. We believe that such a space resembles, metaphorically, a sanctuary. Certain of the qualities of a sanctuary or great cathedral evoke the spiritual and emotional atmosphere we have in mind.

First, in the sanctuary all are invited to gather. For effective processing of conflict, all parties must feel invited and welcomed within the space. The metaphoric room must be large enough to receive all with their diverse and often differing opinions and needs. Second, it must be a space with enough silence that people think well and deeply about what they know and hear. The silence must be deep and long enough that people hear their words held in the vast mystery of the unknown and unknowing. This space helps the participant experience the relative size of individual ideas in relation to the full mystery of God. Third, this space must also create a sense of timelessness and patience, for it will take time to hear well, to think deeply, and to discern directions together. When one considers how long people have held the values or ideas that are being shared and that may be askew with one another, one can appreciate the time it might take for the losses to be grieved so that the future might be embraced. Fourth, this space must reveal the respect owed to creatures of the God who creates in diversity and change. If the participants feel respected, if they feel heard and their sense of self is honored, they will be more motivated to stay connected to the process as well as possible and to support the outcome. Fifth, this space must have room for experimenting with new ideas and the grace of forgiveness when we make mistakes in our understanding or our actions. Communities are sustained over long periods of conflict, change, and loss by the liberating spirit of forgiveness that enables them to deal with the hurt and pain that occurs in emotionally charged human encounters. Sixth, out of this spirit of experimentation and grace grows a vision that gives direction and insight in the church's movement toward the future. Hope is more active in the conflict when there is a commonly held vision of the future that interests and even excites the participants.[1]

What is the work that a congregation needs to do in this sacred space in relation to its conflicts? In the journey of grieving loss within the processing of conflict we believe that there are moments at which insights and discoveries can be made that will help open up a better future. These moments do not happen and then are over. They are revisited over and over again in the journey, and a congregation and its leaders can assist the process by enabling a repetition of the practices that bring these moments to mind. In the largest sense, one we will describe more fully in the next chapter, it is the liturgy of a congregation as it seeks to participate with God's work in the world that provides the holding environment. The liturgy is the central work within the sanctuary. Yet in working with conflict we believe it is important to highlight certain more proximate features of the work of the people that are central to grieving well. We believe that the following ten dimensions of grieving move most deeply within the liturgical rhythm we will later describe. At this point, however, we want to highlight these features in themselves.

Naming Losses

One of the important tasks for a group is to name its losses. When we invite a congregation to change, it is important to remember that every change results in loss. Most of us in the church do not want change even though we know that Jesus said that if we seek to save our lives we will lose them, but if we lose our lives we will find them. We affirm that God acted in the loss of the life of Jesus to redeem the world. We break bread and drink wine to remember the loss that centers our future. We baptize people, speaking words of dying and rising. And yet as congregations who affirm hope in the midst of loss, we struggle with endings. Churches seldom take something away when they add something.

One of the hardest things to do in church is to name something as ended, over, and gone. The reason is that each of these things is an integral part of who we know ourselves to be. If we have learned about ourselves as caring people by practicing compassion in a Sunday school class for forty years, it is hard to let that class go merely because it has shrunk to only four members. The community of people who helped us know ourselves as caring dies out, and part of us dies. Everything that we do is important or has been important to someone. And to stop doing something important for the sake of doing something else important is very difficult.

The conflict in Faith Church was intensified by the inability of some in the congregation to accept the fact that their former minister, Pastor Joe, was no longer their leader. The regular presence of his wife in the church's life kept alive his presence. The struggle of the church to accept and deal with Ernest Brown's leadership and preaching was confused by the constant comparison of the work of one who no longer led the congregation with the current minister and his work within the current community. The inability to grieve the end of prior leadership and the former community context made it very difficult to embrace new direction and new ways of doing things.

We know that new life has a better chance of growing if a space has been cleared for its emergence. Gardeners tell us that when plants grow too thickly, there is no room for new growth. Unless plants and shrubs are pruned, new life cannot grow. Empty space is necessary for something new to happen. Even though it is difficult to give up parts of our lives that we value for the possibility of new life, we must do it.

Since loss is important for new life, leaders and followers need not only to challenge one another to explore new life but also to help one another name the losses that come from giving up the old life. Naming must happen over and over around each loss because of the multilayered dimension of loss. In First Community Church the congregation had been losing members. Loss of members is more than simply the presence of fewer people to support the budget. Were First Community Church members to begin listing the multiple losses they experienced with the shrinking membership, not only would they have discovered the complexity of their situation, but also they would have realized that addressing the losses was a longer and more difficult process than they thought. They would have been able to see that addressing the situation would require more than simply getting a new minister who could attract younger members.

Leaders can help people make lists of losses that come when change is made. They can also help people distinguish between what will be lost and what they only fear will be lost. They should also revisit this naming process repeatedly during the journey of change to allow people to add to or subtract from the list of loss because we don't always know at the beginning all the implications of the change. These losses, when noticed and acknowledged, lose some of their power to later return and deplete the energy needed to move forward.

When people name their multiple losses, they begin to discover the multiple things that have to be attended to if they are to learn to live again in the absence of those losses. If a church thinks the loss of members is only a matter of numbers, it will think that getting a pastor who can attract more people is the solution to their problem. But if the members realize that the loss of members also means the loss of their own sense of themselves, the loss of their sense of power and influence, the loss of a spirit of energy that comes from large groups of people sitting side by side in the sanctuary, the loss of personal friends whom they have come to love, and so on, they will discover that learning to live again in the absence of these people will require other actions than simply replacing the minister. This awareness can lead to a more realistic strategy to help the congregation gain vitality in its new situation.

However, there is another value present when people discover the full cost of decisions that result in change and loss. The more people can have a clear sense of the costs of a change, the more likely they are to carry it through. However, if they get inspired by some vision and get excited about it and start with a great deal of energy but then keep encountering more costs than they realized were a part of the price, they may be inclined to give up before the change is fully implemented. The bookshelves of many churches are the resting place for many a long-range plan that never went anywhere. Exploring the cost is important if a congregation wants to fulfill its vision and its goals.

Feeling Pain

People who want change or who embrace change sometimes act to shame those who resist the change. Both the reformers and those who do not want to reform often see change as a sign that there is something wrong with people who hold to the old ways. Reformers are sometimes inclined to try to bring those persons who resist change on board with the change by shaming them into it. One of the popular bumper stickers of church reformers is: "Do you know what the seven last words of the church are? We never did it that way before." The implication is that those who resist change will be responsible for the death of the church.

We do not see resistance to change as an indication of something wrong with the people who do not want change. Rather, we see it as the presence of deeply held values that are possibly threatened by the change. Change is about loss. So, rather than shaming persons for feeling pain when we talk about taking something away, we ought to respect their feelings by honoring what it is that is being lost. By paying attention, we may discover in their resistance something that, when we consider it well, we may not want to lose. Likewise, trying to talk people out of their pain by suggesting what a wonderful thing can happen in the absence of what they think is important is to diminish them as persons. By discounting their feelings, you discount them. And in the church, many people have been discounted by leaders and fellow worshipers who, in their anger and frustration over people's reluctance to change, devalue their feelings. There are many wounded refugees from religious institutions who wander outside the church because when they were vulnerable over the loss of something that was important to them, they were shamed and ridiculed for being "troublemakers."

Troublemakers may be people who have experienced the loss of face. We each have ways in which we want to be known. When a conflict "becomes personal" and the differences between people move into an attack on the character of the people rather than on a difference of belief, people are likely to "lose face." They feel embarrassed or ashamed. They feel that they are not seen as they want themselves to be seen. They may feel that the response of others to their ideas reflects the others' opinion that they are stupid or uncaring. They will then become defensive, and often their ability to adjust their position on the issue is blocked by their desire to defend their integrity. Congregations in conflict must be aware of the danger of the loss of face and must work to offer face-saving experiences. When people resist change, paying careful attention to what they are saying and showing respect for their opinions, even while not necessarily agreeing, can help those people not lose face in the conflict.[2]

If we take time to help people feel their pain by creating a safe place for people to name and feel their losses, the individuals and the church can make some significant discoveries about their identity as a group. Pain teaches us what matters and what we value. We do not feel pain over loss of something that isn't of value to us. If we are going to walk with people through change, our attention to their pain will help us discover what they value in who they are. By helping people name their loss and feel their pain, we discover what sacred values the church has nurtured in the past. Drawing on those values as we try to live in the future often gives energy and power to that new life.

When Urban Chapel moved toward the decision of building a new sanctuary or a community center, there was much discussion about the values reflected in each decision. Each side reflected values that had been nurtured by the church's life historically. Had the leaders of the church led the church in exploring what each was going to lose and how it felt to them to lose what they considered to be of highest value, they might have been able to help one another begin to grieve the losses that were coming. Instead of attending to those kinds of feelings along the way, the feelings of pain mounted and resulted in people attacking and blaming one another, and the heated differences became a painful tool of division. Attending to the feelings of loss and pain that accompany change does take more time, but the potential for success is improved if people feel heard and known rather than discounted and ignored.

It is very helpful to know what the people in the church value. When we know this, we can attend to those values and see if there are new ways to acknowledge and nurture those values. It is possible to help people discover that the church does honor them by nurturing those values in other areas of the church's life. If people know that their values will be attended to, even if they are not addressed exactly as they have been in the past, the people are more likely to offer support for the change. Then, when we are suggesting changes for the future, we can show them how their values are reflected in this new way of interacting with the world.

Leaders who feel the pain with others are more trustworthy as leaders. Followers who feel the pain of others are also more trustworthy. Mutual levels of trust and respect within a community result in a kind of creative cocreation of a space in which the vulnerability required for feeling the pain of loss is more richly possible.

The leader who seeks to guide transformation must also have patience. Deeply held values are woven tightly into the fabric of individual and congregational identity. Ritual practices in personal habits and congregational systems have shaped the identity of persons over long stretches of time. To name and experience the pain of the multiple losses that occur in change requires steadfast presence and patience on the part of those guiding the transformation process.

Being Angry

Feelings of anger are frequently the first clue leaders have that people are fearing loss. Anger will often be focused on the persons they believe are responsible for the losses. Anger is a response to threat and fragmentation of the self, as we discussed in chapter 3. When people feel that their identity or what they love or deeply value is being threatened, their rage will begin to stir. This anger is energy (adrenaline) that can lead to a fight-flight response. It will be used to create alienation from those who pose the threat or to destroy that which is believed to pose a threat. Anger within the system can function to weaken the system from within—with some members in the system striking out at others. The energy that could be harnessed for fulfilling their hopes of the future ends up being dissipated or destructive. Or the church system can be weakened by its members leaving the church in order to protect themselves from their fear and anxiety. The absence of these people reduces the energy and resources that could help the church achieve its goals in the future. Or sometimes the energy that is generated in anger is used to simply stop the institution from moving at all, paralyzing it in hopes of protecting it from making a mistake that could be fatal to its existence.

Many people in church seek to avoid the anger they feel when they deal with one another in congregations. Since anger is the energy that encourages people to fight to defend what they value or to run from those who would take it away, it is a force that is hard to control or guide. Often pastors, such as Reverend Walsh at First Community Church, have a history of avoiding conflict or employing a passive-aggressive response to the challenge. In the congregation there are diverse ways in which people are inclined to deal with their anger, and these complicate the ability to work through it. When these various responses to perceived threats coalesce in the congregation's life, unraveling them and dealing with them is sometimes a challenge.

If anger is fear of loss, the community needs to be present in a way that helps its members feel they are not losing their power to affect what occurs. If the leader has power, and people feel threatened, being close to the leader whom they feel has power can help reduce their anxiety and thus their anger.

In the Urban Church, Pastor Marquis discerned his position and declared it. While clarity on the part of the leader is important, clarity communicated with no room for negotiation can serve to make those who disagree with him feel that their differences of opinion separate them from the ability to influence the future. This sense of powerlessness comes from being divided from one they feel has power, and it can intensify their anger and encourage them to act out by withholding their support or leaving the church. If Pastor Marquis could have kept from feeling that their difference from him was a personal attack and a challenge to his authority, maybe he could have offered leadership that would have allowed those who opposed his decision to feel as if they didn't have to threaten to leave.

Another role of the leader in engaging this anger is to help reframe the issues in a way that help people see them as "our" issues, not "us and them" issues. When we are offended, we are tempted to separate ourselves from those who hurt us. If a leader can help us understand the position held by the other, we might be less likely to try to hurt them. But if a group or subgroup collapses into the "us and them" paranoid-schizoid state of mind, it will be easier to strike out at the other or to leave the other than if the group considers that there is something about us that needs attention.

Since anger is about loss of security and identity, it also engages people's fear of abandonment. If the energy we feel in anger gets used to drive us apart or to destroy the other who threatens what we value, we as leaders need to find ways to help people stay connected in their differences. Sometimes that connection is made by the pastor staying connected to people on both sides of any issue. If Reverend Walsh had been able to stay emotionally connected to those who were seeking her resignation and had allowed them to articulate their fears and losses, staying connected might have helped them process the intensity of their feelings and anxieties and allowed them to explore other alternatives for addressing their fears.

Remembering

When change occurs, people lose something. Change separates people from part of who they know themselves to be. As observed in chapter 3, the familiar may be something that gives them a positive sense of themselves, a feeling of worth or recognition. It may be a sense of home, security, or efficacy. It may be a compass point that helps orient them and give them a sense of direction.

Churches do not always realize and acknowledge the power of what has changed. People who are struggling against the change are often encouraged to "forget the past and move on." People who offer such advice fail to recognize that deeply held values cannot simply be forgotten. Willing ourselves to forget is about as effective as a child willing herself to stop sucking her thumb. The unconscious response of a child to anxiety causes the body to unthinkingly stick the thumb in the mouth. To tell someone in the church to simply forget the past is to assume that one can "unknow" who he or she once was.

Anyone who has lost a job or a partner or a child knows how the presence of the past isn't simply erased by willful thought. The past—the powerful ritualized and embodied values that have shaped who we are—resides within us and doesn't simply disappear because we think it should. The past must be remembered and integrated into the fullness of who we are becoming. In that way, there is integrity and wholeness in who we are becoming.

This understanding seems to be contrary to the thoughts of some who study the way the world is becoming and who advise that forgetfulness is the greatest virtue for living in these "liquid times." Zygmunt Bauman has defined the times we live in as liquid. The rapid change in our world creates an almost contemporaneous obsolescence. We learn how to live in the current time, and then things change, and the skills we learned for that time no longer work in this time. We must forget what we have known so we can live effectively in the future.[3]

We believe that a better way to move into the future is for a leader not to encourage people to forget but to encourage them to remember. She needs to help a congregation remember its past well enough that it becomes integrated into the community it is becoming. The new identity of the body finds its roots in the history of its forbears. It may be necessary for the church to forget certain skills and ways of doing things in order to adapt itself to serve the changing world, but at the core, remembering and grieving function better to sustain the vital witness to its mission of compassion and justice.

For the past to be well remembered and integrated into the future requires that the people accept the past as past, the loss as loss. The Cassville congregation tried to move into the future after the retirement of their longtime minister. But the former minister and his wife remained active in the congregation and complicated the process of remembering well. Thoughtful remembrances of what has been define the process of shrinking the past into a more mobile, pocket-sized presence so it can accompany the congregation into the future without controlling the shape of that future. The process of memorializing the past is characterized by the complex and rich emotional life of the present shrinking to a portable memorial to bless but not define the future.

Remembering long and well is also about rehumanizing the past. Frequently, the past, when it is gone, takes on divine qualities. Many congregations have memories of pastors that elevate those pastors to near sainthood. They become symbols of the way God intends a pastor to be. They are often associated with better times for the church. They sometimes take on a larger-than-life quality, making it virtually impossible for any living pastor to compete. This was the case at Faith Church. Pastor Joe's longtime ministry among the people created a deep and abiding presence. For many people, he defined what it was to be a minister. He set the standard. In his absence from leadership in the congregation, his presence was felt to be much larger, and he became idealized. A congregation that is in the process of learning to live again in the absence of a beloved pastor need to remember that pastor and that time well enough that its humanity returns. When members of a congregation are honest, they will not simply remember the good things about the past but also will remember the struggles and sufferings. The past will look more like humans struggling with themselves and the world in the presence of the Divine. The more honest we are about the past, the more honest we can be about the current situation in which we find ourselves and the more we can accept a "human leader" who replaces the idealized images of the leaders of the past.

When people lose something for the sake of something new, they must be guided in their remembrance of what it is that is lost. One minister asked her congregation to tell the stories of the church's history. She posted sheets of paper around the walls of the fellowship hall. Each flip-chart-sized sheet represented a ten-year period. She asked the members to go around and write words that represented events they had heard happened in that decade. Stories were then told that helped the people remember where they came from. Once they discovered that they and others had suffered many losses in their history, they were open to considering what might be lost now. And once they saw the relationship between what they lost and what it was they discovered beyond the loss, they were more open to the possibility that the changes being proposed would open richer and better ways of being in the future.

However, remembering takes time. Religious communities' awareness of how powerful memory is can be seen by the ritualized way it is done. Built into the church's life and liturgy are constant references to the past. Reading and referencing Scripture in discussions about who we are and what we should be doing are frequent occurrences. Stories that take on normative power are declared sacred, and remembering them gives shape and structure to the identity of the community of faith. Religious people tend to give regular time to the acts of remembering.

Earlier work in the area of loss and bereavement seemed to assume that the result of effective grieving was the disappearance of the past for the sake of a new future. However, more recent studies suggest that effective grieving results in the ability to reposition the memory so that what is lost no longer occupies such an emotionally charged position in the self.[4] In the revisiting of the past, the self remembers the self anew based on how those stories of the past intersect with the emerging stories of the new context of the individual.

This process is true in churches as well. The past is an integral part of who we continue to become. Churches who grieve well and who are in a constant state of transformation are ones who ritually revisit their past and allow it to continually shape and reshape their future even as the future continues to shape and reshape their memories of the past. The interaction of memory and the past creates the vitality for an ever-forming and reforming of the organization and the individuals in the church.

This revisiting of the past can be done both liturgically (as we will explore in the next chapter) and also institutionally as a church has annual "homecoming" days or anniversary celebrations. It can be done with any discussion in committees or board meetings as individuals remember experiences of their past that may help contribute to understanding how the church might move forward even as it shapes the direction the church decides to take.

In a community in change and transition, time spent in remembering how things have been is time well spent. Remembering helps people mentalize. It helps them take their affective experience and give it name. Remembering in community gives power to the individual memory. By asking people to remember, we honor who they have been and what gives their life meaning in the present. In this way the past is metabolized in the present.

Leaders in institutions validate people by asking them to remember rather than discounting their past by asking them to forget. As Freud knew, to remember well is not to repeat but to rework and transform what is remembered toward a new future.[5] People who have a sense of confidence in themselves because they are affirmed in what they have been will have more energy for acting in the future toward what they might become.

Feeling Guilt and Shame

Another emotional response that might be elicited in the midst of conflict and change is that of shame and guilt. For instance, when something that is valued disappears, we have a tendency to seek out reasons for the loss. When a church starts losing members, we want to know why. Someone must be responsible. Someone is to blame. People sometimes feel that they have either done or not done something (guilt) that resulted in this loss. They assume that they had the ability to do or not do that "something," resulting in the guilt of omission or commission. Other times, they feel that there is something simply inadequate or wrong about the character of the church or themselves (shame). In the midst of conflict and loss they feel that they are just not enough.

When shame and guilt are activated, it can contribute to the intensity of conflict. Sometimes the blame is focused on the pastor. Reverend Walsh was called to First Community Church partly because some in the church believed that a younger person with a family would attract younger people. When this didn't happen, some blamed Reverend Walsh's lack of commitment to the church as reflected in her family's not joining. Reverend Walsh was the offending party and became the focus of much blame. But Reverend Walsh also felt guilt within herself. The conflict that the congregation was engaged in was about the loss of dreams and expectations. Their hopes for a "family" church somehow were not being realized. Reverend Walsh's dreams were not being realized either. "Maybe I should have considered my family's desires more. Maybe I could have done something to help my family make the move." She was also shamed and felt that she just might not be enough for them. When we make decisions that change the context we live in and there are problems with the outcome, we are likely to try to find someone to blame. And the guilty party may be ourselves.

Since shame and guilt seem so closely tied to each other, it can be helpful to differentiate between them so that we can attend to the intensity of feelings and focus the energy that may recruit people into different camps. Guilt has a way of expanding and assigning blame. The pastor is frequently the one who receives the blame and thus is the center of the conflict. The congregation or a subgroup within the congregation assigns the guilt. When the conflict intensifies, either those who side with the pastor are responsible, or those who attack the pastor are the ones guilty of causing the problems. In cases such as this, a community of faith must create a space in which leader and follower alike can feel and name the guilt. Changes over which no one had control may be what caused the loss. In naming the loss and identifying the multiple factors that contribute to changes that result in that loss, the congregation can clarify and better understand the circumstances that created their pain. If Barbara Cooper at Faith Church could have helped focus the conversation on the larger context and the changes that had occurred in the community, the people might have been able to see that the issue wasn't all about the pastor. If the loss of the role that the previous pastor played could have

113

been identified and named honestly, the community might have seen that the current pastor was not totally responsible for the lack of spiritual energy.

Communities of faith must also help people explore how shame is functioning to intensify the emotions in a conflict. If a church simply feels that it is not enough and is not worthy of a pastor's leadership or wonders why "anyone would want to join this church," it needs to deal with a more basic issue of self-worth. Knowing and naming the sense of guilt or discovering how shame underlies some of the conflict helps us discover our need for grace. Reverend Walsh felt more responsibility for the problems than she might have if she had clarified the multiple losses that all were feeling. Had she been clear about her responsibility and her mistakes, she could have been open to forgiveness for particular decisions. But if she felt responsible for more than what she had power over, forgiveness might have been difficult to receive.

Forgiving

Forgiving is being freed from the power of the pain of the past for the sake of the future. This is a freeing spirit that opens persons to act new ways in the future. If we don't exercise a forgiving attitude toward the past that has not turned out the way we wanted, either we will try to recreate the past so that we don't have to lose it, or we will try to escape it by creating something entirely new. Neither is ever fully possible. Forgiving creates an arena in which we are free to live in the present and take the wisdom of the past and let it enrich our decisions about the future. Sometimes forgiving is focused on personal or corporate sin and sometimes simply on the limitations and vulnerability of human life.

In this transforming process of grieving loss, we use the word *forgiving* rather than the word *forgiveness*. We believe that the process of becoming free from the power of the pain of the past is an evolutionary process and that it is a continuing process even as we act to live in new ways. We believe we can act toward a new future even while the pain of the past is operative in our lives. *Forgiveness* implies that something is accomplished or finished. We believe that becoming free for the future is more a gift that comes as the result of the hard work of grieving rather than something that one is able to will and achieve. The power of the pain of the past will always reside somewhere within the person or institution where the pain has been experienced; therefore, *forgiving* represents an ongoing task. Rather than criticize ourselves for not having fully forgiven, we can celebrate the slow and subtle movements toward new life. Becoming free from the power of that pain of loss begins when persons or churches begin to feel stronger and are not as intensely threatened by the loss that they experienced. As the congregation weathers the changes and the emotions and feelings of anger and pain, it might discover that it has more resilience than it thought at first. As the members draw together, remembering what life was like and what changes are taking place around them and within them, they gain the strength of connection with others who have a common history and memory. As they name their feelings of guilt and shame over what they might have done differently, they discover in the mutual vulnerability a common spirit of humility and humanity. As they grow in strength together, the pain of the loss begins to lose its grip on them, and they discover new energy for new life. This is the work of the spirit of forgiving.

The community needs to help people feel secure together so they can forgive the past for changing. The liturgical context is one of those places where it is natural to remind the congregation that we are forgiven. The safety and security of the ritual practices of worship in which people are familiar with confession and grace help people practice the process of forgiving that lead to new possibilities in life. When we do not feel as threatened by the change, when we know ourselves to be more than what it is that is lost, we are freed from the control of the fear or the pain and can live with more energy in the present and the future.

Giving Thanks

As a congregation goes through the process of discovering its life by paying attention to the various parts of the process of grieving, it comes to an awareness that there were gifts in the past. It is important to go through these parts of the process because if we don't, the pain and anger of the past can blind us to the truth about the past and, ironically, bind us to that past.

Congregations will frequently get stuck in the trauma of the past and will be unable to access the full story of their life that includes both pain and blessing, fear and security, loss and gain. When dissociation, which initially functions to allow a group to tolerate the suffering of trauma, becomes permanently planted in the heart of a community and the trauma is not remembered well, the group may be unable to move into an embrace of the giftedness of the future. But when a congregation does the work that honors the memory and those who hold it, identifying and mourning the losses that they have experienced and are experiencing, then they are able to glimpse the gifts of life that were in their life before as well as possible gifts in the loss itself. This awareness of the gifts that were part of what has been opens the mind to consider the possibility that there may be gifts in the potential that is there because of the losses created by changes. This is not true for all losses. But when it is true, it helps reduce fear. If the past changes produce some gifts for us to remember, then we are opened to look for the new things as gifts that we didn't anticipate receiving until we experienced the loss.

Leading an institution into the future requires that its members discover a spirit of gratitude. This opens the people to more energy. Church leaders are reminded weekly of the gifts of life that are received in the midst of pain and sacrifice as they liturgically offer their gifts for the sake of the world. The altar becomes a place where, in the practice of bringing gifts that are the result of the breaking of our lives and offering these broken parts of ourselves to God, we see gifts of grace and new life that are possible for us and for the world. God's self-giving that has become a gift to us and our self-giving that becomes a gift to the world open our eyes to the gifted nature of existence. It sets the table for our hearts to embrace the world in gratitude.

Playing

When the power of the past to control our future is weakened by the process of grieving loss, people can start imagining a new way of being. Emerging energy can enter into a process of reinventing the future in the absence of the way things used to be. The church members can try new things. Because the present and future worlds are different from the world in which the conflict and loss occurred, no one can know for sure what the community can become. They can develop a capacity to experiment and then adapt when they learn something from their experience. They can play.

To play requires a sense of safety. To play means that we are going to experiment. It means that we will make mistakes but that we will arrange the experimentation so that if things don't work out it won't destroy the church. Jane Pooley,[6] in her discussion of coaching executives leading organizational change, talks of the importance of creating a safe place for people to play with new ideas. She says that it is as important for adults as it is for children to develop the capacity to symbolize inner thoughts and feelings. Play is the space in which we can be visualize and explore alternative ways of responding to the world without having to be held accountable for them within a given situation.

Playing requires the grace to make mistakes without becoming our mistakes. It requires imagination that is freed from the bonds of the past so new ways of living can take shape in the mind and soul. Pooley says, "It is only in an environment that can accept mistakes that people learn to tolerate and digest their experiences and to think and reflect without being compelled into knee-jerk reactions."[7] When memory and imagination wrestle with each other, some people may be hurt. There will be pain as it becomes clear that things will have to change and that some losses will be experienced. In the changing context of doing ministry, some efforts will succeed and some will fail. Grace for forgiving the mistakes is an essential component of learning from our experience and shaping new life in the absence of the old.

One of the ways this playful attitude can work as a congregation anticipates making changes is to role-play and experiment with the outcome of the change. As the Urban Chapel anticipated decisions about its future capital campaign, leaders could have gathered and imagined how people might respond to the different strategies. They could have invited people to share what it might feel like if each decision was made. They might have created a setting in which those who were against the sanctuary would hear the hopes of those who were for it. Those who were for the community center could share the hopes and fears related to their dreams.

To lead an institution in change, one has to create a sense of security on the part of the people in it so that they are free to learn from their experience. Participants need to feel that there is freedom to be inventive and that the organization will not collapse if the experiment fails. They need to know that the costs of learning from experience are survivable.[8] They also need to know that there is more than one way to move ahead in relationship to the world in which the institution is living its mission. There are multiple dimensions to a church's context. Therefore, mission and ministry can take various forms and still be faithful. Experimenting with different responses to the context can help them discover the few ministries that best represent the passions and interests of the people who make up the congregation.

Following a crisis in which loss has been experienced, new options might emerge that persons didn't see before. The vision of the future that is so central for life to flourish emerges from the soil of graceful play. When people can honestly explore who they have been and what their changing cultural context is becoming, new directions can begin to take form. One church in the West found itself graying quickly. Most of the members were above the age of sixty. The response of the congregation was to get a younger minister who would "attract" younger families. The losses of their lives were pressing in, and they were looking for hope that their congregation would not die. The only way they could see to keep that from happening was to focus on new and younger people.

However, the young minister who came in had a different idea. With his influence and sharing of ideas, they decided that the best thing to do was to create vital ministry to and with those who were in the congregation. The church started focusing on care for the older population. At first this seemed a puzzling solution to the problem of developing a more multigenerational church, but the church appreciated the young pastor's pastoral care. The word got around the community, and other older adults began to come to the church. And then the word got around to the adult children of these aging parents that there was a church committed to the ministry to persons they loved. And they started showing up to see what kind of place this was. Younger families with children began to join the church because of the care given the aging population.

The playful spirit of imagination is essential if a congregation is going to emerge from the pain of its significant losses to discover the new life that is seeded in the womb of its own congregational life. They can be surprised by the gifts of grace in the future.

Practicing

When a church has been in conflict and is grieving its way toward a new future, it must make some decisions about its direction. When it does, it must put those decisions into practice. This requires assessment of the resources of the institution and the commitment of its members. When decisions are made, then commitment to practicing the new must take precedence over continued practice of the old. Human, financial, emotional, and spiritual resources that once flowed in one direction must now begin to flow into the new commitments that the organization has made. This practice of the new will be difficult at times. It is hard to practice new skills when you would rather be doing things that were not as demanding, that were more familiar. But the persistent practice of new directions and skills will eventually result in feelings of confidence and comfort in this new identity.

At this point in the process of living into the new reality, leaders and followers must regularly remind themselves of the commitments they have made. The stories of their common life, of the losses that have occurred both within the church and within the community and culture in which the church ministers, must be rehearsed. We often lose track of the life we have lived and the experiences that we have been given. We fail to remember and honor the hard work of grieving that has shaped us and helped move us forward. Leaders must help set aside time for the congregation to celebrate its steps, however halting, toward a new way of life. Praise and affirmation help encourage us in times when we want to give up and give in to hopelessness. This is further developed in the next chapter.

Through the grieving process, a congregation learns truths about itself and what its character is. These discoveries need to be metabolized into the church's practices. A congregational leader's work with the body as a whole is to help the church develop systems that normalize the new practices it has developed. Leaders and followers can build into their practice the liturgical rhythm of revisiting the issues of change and loss, helping people stay in touch with what matters, what they and others might be losing as the church evolves into its new way of being, and how they are growing spiritually toward the new life. An urban church that has had a steady decline in membership and ministry has discovered a new breath of life. Its members decided that the old system of governance just didn't work with the small number of people who were left. They created a new structure that allowed for some members to be freed up to fan sparks of new ideas. But they were aware that with a smaller governing board, some would feel left out. The loss of contact and influence would be a problem. They decided that they would have occasional gatherings shaped by the World Cafe model of group life. On important issues that they knew were of keen interest to some of the members, they would hold guided conversations that invited input from everyone. The expressions of fear, hope, pain, and vision would be taken seriously by the leaders as they made plans for the future. And if the leaders perceived that one gathering was not enough, they would structure another one in a couple of months until they felt that everyone had expressed themselves and had felt heard.

This is one of the many ways for a church that has done the hard work of grieving loss well to take what it has learned from its experience and build a system that perpetuates values that are reflected in its new practices. It is a way to attend to the feelings of people who care deeply and who need to process the losses that are present in the changes that are happening.

Becoming New

Churches morph into new life. They do not emerge fully formed and functional. They slowly build and take on new character. The new people, the new context, the new structure, and the new ministries reshape the character of the organization. Awareness of this new reality is frequently slow to materialize. It often requires some time for people within the institution to become aware that a new thing is emerging.

One of the most important leadership functions that is necessary at this point in the grieving process is that of naming and pointing out the new realities as they emerge. The new seldom emerges full-blown. It grows in fits and starts. In the midst of the emotional chaos of change and growth, it is often hard to notice the subtle changes that have emerged. The energy required to work through the changes and to grieve the loss of the stability of the past sometimes exhausts an organization, and no one even notices the transformation that has taken place. When laity or clergy emerge and witness to the new, they become leaders into the future. Their bearing witness to the new thing that God is doing can become the occasion for celebration and joy. When this new thing is noticed and celebrated, members can work together to nurture its growth.

It is important that this kind of naming of the new reality happens frequently. Congregations are peopled by individuals who have many claims and responsibilities. In the diverse tugs on their time, they lose track of the congregational narrative. They feel and experience the narrow and individual concerns of their own lives. Leaders within the church have the responsibility to keep the whole story before the people. People who have a fuller picture of where the church has been and how it is moving toward where it is going feel more a part of the new and emerging life.

Facilitating the telling and retelling of the story is part of the leader's role as the congregation emerges into a new way of being.

When a church has been living one way for decades and then tries to recreate itself for a new context for ministry, the temptation is for the old ways to resist and pull people back to them. When the conflict and tension create tough times in the birthing of a new way of being, leaders will be called upon to help these new practices become more engrained in the consciousness and memory of the people. Telling and retelling the story is the way this new community can be formed and strengthened.

We have been describing moments in the journey of grieving loss that can offer insights into the conflict that a congregation is experiencing. We believe that this process is not simply one that helps a congregation deal with intense and momentary conflict but also that can give shape and form to the way the congregation functions in its normal routine of processing life. If the community practices attention to the above ten dimensions of discovery when it is dealing with less intense changes, it may discover a way of grieving loss that does not develop into an explosive situation. If a congregation teaches these practices in workshops and educational events, people may develop them as skills that they can use not only in congregational life but also within their own personal lives when conflict and loss take place. If people are given insights related to this grieving process *and* gain skills in attending to this process by practicing them in community, this knowledge will be more available to them when emotions get high than if they don't understand what is happening.

Along with educational events that are created to help develop these insights and skills, we also believe that most congregations already potentially practice this process on a weekly basis. We believe that the formal liturgical practices of worship and preaching are fundamentally the creation of a community that is formed by this process. We develop this idea in the next chapter.

CHAPTER 6

Preaching and Practicing Liturgy: Resources for Leading Congregations in Conflict

Truth, like love and sleep, resists approaches that are too intense.
—W. H. Auden

A s we have worked our way through this book, we have established that conflict is, in and of itself, not a bad thing. We believe that it is not only an inevitable part of life but also a source of vitality and energy in life. We have shown how it reflects the incredible beauty and diversity of creation, and we have suggested that the way to process conflict in congregations for the purpose of life and blessing is to help people in the church grieve the losses that underlie conflict. Conflict can best contribute to renewal and transformation when it is not avoided but when people *move more fully into it* and discover what it might offer for their moving toward a new place in their future. Leaders who are effective at helping congregations grieve their losses are those who are present in the community with a "heart of flesh." They are people who are called by the community to lead them from where they are to where God is calling them to be. Their leadership is formed and developed within the conflicts that are experienced in the liquid context of change as people with diverse insights and experiences work together to find their way forward as a community of faith.

123

In this chapter we will show how leading in conflict toward a transformed future is enhanced by the leader visibly taking and being taken by her role as preacher and leader of worship. We will show how the role of guiding the conversations of the community within the context of the primary work of the church—worshipping God—enables a leader to help a community grieve its losses that result from change and move toward the embrace of the new future to which God is calling it. Although this chapter is not about how liturgy and preaching are used to lead a congregation in the midst of intense conflict per se, understanding how liturgy and preaching function within the ongoing life of a church to facilitate people's grieving their personal and corporate losses in order to move forward with life is essential. Understanding liturgy in this way can contribute to the community's ability to see how the church's worship practices create a frame for dealing with the more heated conflicts that arise. Conflicts within the liturgical readings and the explication of those conflicts in preaching lay the groundwork for how one can lead in conflict when people in the congregation become askew.

Liturgy and Formation

For humans to function within the Christian community well— that is, for people to embrace and be embraced by Divine energy and direction for the sake of the blessing of the world—we need to have access to two primary forces: stability and change. Preaching and liturgy contribute to the congregation's having access to these two forces. Predictability is the ground on which we live that provides the sense of continuity and identity necessary for a community of faith. To that end, we tell the stories of our ancestors to ourselves and our children. The stories of our ancestors and the stories of our own lives that we rehearse and remember are what give us a sense of who we are. This sense of self, both individually and within the community, is essential so that we don't have to reinvent ourselves each moment of each day. These stories differentiate us from others who have different stories. They represent something of the unique experience of the individual as he lives within the given context of life.

124

These stories then become ritualized into practices that shape our daily living and give shape and form to who we are. The dependable structure around us helps reinforce the identity that the stories reveal. The repetition of practices creates an embodied memory of the story that gave rise to the ritual.

Each congregation has a set of stories that the community accepts as its canon. The Bible is essentially the set of stories that the church has authorized as the ones that form its identity. Each congregation has those stories from which to choose. Some choose certain stories to give voice to what they value and what their character is. Other congregations choose other stories. Because of the multiplicity and diversity in the Bible, the stories do not always create harmony. Indeed, sometimes they seem to be at odds. Some tell of a God whose mercy is poured out on the just and the unjust. Others tell of a God who separates the sheep and goats, with some going into eternal joy while others go into eternal punishment. Different congregations rehearse different stories to help them know who they are and what is the character of the God they serve

But for churches to have effective groundwork for processing conflict and loss, these diverse stories must be rehearsed. The diversity itself can help congregations access the variety of modes of generating experience that are necessary for human flourishing. If a church focuses only on stories of love and mercy and fails to teach and preach the stories of judgment and fear, the resources for helping a congregation access its depressive mode of knowing will be underdeveloped. If the stories of one side of a moral dilemma are always the focus of preaching, the congregation will grow to believe that the faith is simply a matter of either/or propositions. It will perhaps encourage the congregation to collapse into the paranoid-schizoid mode. When preaching and liturgy faithfully represent the multiple dimensions of the human and Divine realities, people will grow to understand that navigating the future will sometimes be messy and confusing and will require negotiating differences.

Each congregation not only has the common stories of the canon that connect it to other congregations but also has its own individual stories that help give shape to its particular community.

125

Those stories are ones filled with new beginnings and disappointments, joys and pain, gains and losses. They are stories of leaders who helped the congregation flourish and leaders who betrayed the confidence of the congregation. They are tender stories of the homeless helped and families restored. They are stories grounded in the unique soil of each community with all its rich and complex traditions, biases, prejudices, and loves.

As the community tells these stories to itself and to its children, it ritualizes them in the practices of formal and informal gatherings. It develops patterns of behavior that reflect the values embodied in those stories. In the story of Urban Chapel, we became familiar with a congregation that was centered in an inner-city neighborhood. There were hundreds of stories that were created as people lived and worshiped in that particular community. There were stories of need and hope that people living in the church and around the church told one another and their children. Some of those stories were so powerful and life-shaping that they called forth practices by the church that resulted in Pastor Marquis giving this litany of achievements: an after-school program for mentoring young African American males and females, a marriage enrichment program, a job bank, and nine hundred people in church each Sunday. These were programs that helped people create a sense of identity—people whose character was ritualized by these practices. The practices of the church created a sense of stability and permanence. They could count on this identity.

But within a world of constant change, a church must not only rest within its identity but also always be evaluating its work within the emerging community around it so it can adapt to the fluid nature of reality and continue to be effective in its mission and ministry. The ability to change is a critical part of what it means to be a faithful people of a living God. God and the world together continually cocreate a new matrix for ministry, and if a congregation is going to serve the changing world, it must change as well. The adventure of discovering new things and new gifts within God's emerging world is part of the joy of being a Christian community.

The Liturgy as Container

We believe that liturgy and preaching are the constant resources that congregational leaders have to help people explore the changes, discover the losses, grieve those losses, and develop new rituals and practices out of the new stories of their life to become the new creatures God needs to bless the new world. Here is how we think that works.

Liturgy is the container that holds the community of faith while it works out how to live together to bless the world in the name of Christ. It is a part of the boundary-forming activity of the community that is accessed in its embodied form by the members' autistic-contiguous state of mind. This can be illustrated by a story from Dan Moseley's book *Healing Relationships: A Preaching Model*:

It was Saturday morning and I was in a mega-bookstore. I went to the children's section to get a birthday present for one of my grand-daughters. I asked the clerk for the book and while she was search-ing for it, I happened onto a section of the store where parents were sitting in bright plastic beanbag chairs holding children on their laps. They were reading stories to the children. It was then that I realized that this picture of parents and children and books was a model for the way liturgy and preaching work within congregations.

You see, the children can sit with safety on the lap of their parents and feel the security of the parents' arms holding them and the heartbeats against their backs, and it is there that the parents can read the children stories about wolves and witches and the children can face their fears. They can face their fears in the lap of security and safety. They can feel their heartbeat increase as they hear of the chase and they can feel themselves drawn to courage as they feel safe in the arms of the parents.

I came to understand how the liturgy of congregations is like the lap of the parent. It holds the listener [and preacher] in a safe and secure setting while the preacher [and listener are introduced] . . . to the strange and scary world of what it is to be a person of faith who serves the God of the Hebrew people and the God of Jesus Christ. The human heart's desire to grow requires both safety and adven-ture. The liturgy provides the safety while the preaching provides the adventure.[1]

The sense of stability and safety provided by the liturgy is grounded in its familiarity and its constant rehearsal. The liturgical year varies in different communities of faith. Some follow a year that explores the birth, life, death, and resurrection of Jesus followed by the giving of the Spirit, the birth of the church, and the ordinary time when the life and ministry of church are explored through other stories of the Scriptures. This liturgy, rehearsed year after year, becomes predictable. People can count on it. When they participate in the community at a given season, they can count on a given focus at that time and on getting essentially the whole story over a period of time. Other churches have a liturgical year that might include a more secular calendar. They remember the birth of a nation on Independence Day, the good labor in early September, the first Thanksgiving meal in November, the new year in January, the presidents in February, and the fallen soldiers in May. There is a predictable pattern that holds the worshiper within the calendar, that helps make sense of the mundane, and that creates a metastory in which our mini stories have some meaning. We come to count on this order and routine, and this dependable pattern helps reduce our anxiety.

The repetition of the liturgical pattern is the way the symbols of our faith are formed and become sacred in their power. Individuals and communities must develop symbols that represent the stories that form who they are. Some of the symbols are literary—words that are rich and complex and full of multiple meanings. Words such as *God* and *church* and *Holy Spirit* all represent far more than the words themselves. Other symbols are tactile: cross, table, baptismal font. These symbols become more than their material makeup. Their presence, their location in the liturgical space and in the liturgy, and their complex and rich meaning carried through history become powerful formulas for the shaping of the Christian identity.

But liturgy is not only about predictable patterns that help create stability. The liturgy in and of itself contains introductions to strangers as Scripture readings reveal the lives of people whose commitments and social structures are foreign and maybe even offensive to us. The constant presence of these persons from an alien culture who acted in ways that violate many of our own cultural values is disquieting to those who participate in the liturgy.

This hospitality to the stranger within the liturgy is a leavening energy for new life even as the ritual practice of memory makes us feel safe enough to tolerate the dissonance of the stranger. This paradox will be explored more when we examine the classic worship liturgy that gives shape to the Christian community.

Just as the liturgy contains the presence of strangers from other cultures with values different from our own, liturgy also can function to make the presence of the Holy less frightening and painful. The God of the Hebrews and of the Christ is an astonishing and powerful presence whose encounter with our lives is not always pleasing. God's creative energy often results in the wiping away of that which we cherish. The presence of God in the power of death within a family is awful and confusing, powerful and disorienting. The liturgy of the church invites the community to come up against that death and power on a regular basis, rehearsing the pain and the hope that is encountered within those holy terrors and giving us language with which to speak to one another about it and a framework within which we can perceive it in varying ways. By rehearsing these less comfortable stories of God and God's world with a community of people whose commitments reflect our own journey, we might gain a sense of courage that comes from not being in this encounter alone. The losses that come to us in the holy terror of our encounters with the God of creation are experienced in a community of steadfast support that helps us contain our anxiety and grieve well.

The practice of liturgy also helps keep the faithful connected to the ways in which diversity is the nature of the creative spirit. The liturgical year, with its various readings from the canon, continually confronts the participant with the experience of different ways of experiencing the Holy and of naming the activity of God in the world. We experience the God who comes as an infant, the God who suffers death on a cross, the God who lives within the laws created to provide order to a community, and the God who moves like the wind—unpredictable and wild. We experience God as one who blesses monarchs and who participates in their fall, one who uses prophets and also the enemies of God's people to achieve Divine purposes. We see communities of the faithful sharing generously with one another and arguing violently with one another. We see the work of God moving through the varieties of gifts to move creation toward more just and loving relationships. When congregations are grounded in and nurtured by the rehearsal of the liturgical year with its diverse encounters with the Holy, they become familiar with conflict and change, with diversity and difference. This ritualistic practice of telling the stories of the faith helps a community learn to live with these differences and not be driven to eliminate them by conflict that divides and separates.

Liturgy and preaching also create a holding place that facilitates learning from our experience. It is hard to learn from our experience, but it is essential in order to move forward fruitfully. Having the capacity to learn from experience requires language to name what is happening to us. How we name it helps us discover clues to how we might process it and what it might mean for us. The language of the church reveals that loss and death are central realities of creation. Empty space created by change and loss of a way of life is seen in the Biblical story as a location in which new life might be discovered and flourish. The Hebrew people discovered a new identity as they wandered in what was for them a place of fear and emptiness. Jesus' death created a space among his disciples in which the Spirit emerged to create a community of faithful people who expanded Jesus' ministry well beyond the small geographical space of Palestine. Therefore, loss is not something that is to be avoided at all cost, and it may very well be a gift to be embraced. This language of faith helps us hold onto hope for the discovery of meaning and purpose in the future that is emerging in the death of the world the way it was known. Without this language to define what is happening to us, we might be tempted to name our experience using the language of culture that sees the purpose of life to acquire all we can, which results in the fear of losing what we value. To name the world that way is to create a practice of living that builds bigger silos and does all it can to keep from losing what one has, rather than to use God-given gifts to work toward a better future for God's world.

Liturgy and Preaching

So, what is the Christian liturgy that gives shape to the community of people who walk with one another through conflict and loss and that helps the people grieve well and open themselves to the new life God is leading them toward?

Aidan Kavanagh in his book *On Liturgical Theology* shares an outline of the liturgical structure of the worship of the medieval church in Europe that basically embodies the components of Christian worship around the globe.[2] He suggests that the practice of this liturgy is at its core the practice of what it means to live the Christian life. We use this paradigm to give shape to how the liturgy and preaching of the church help congregations become vital and alive communities who grieve well and embrace the future as a gift from God.

Gathering

Father Kavanagh indicates that worship begins with gathering. Church would begin early, in the morning, with the priests going to the edges of the community and then walking through the narrow streets, singing and gathering the faithful from throughout the city in a procession toward the cathedral's sanctuary. All of creation was in the processional, sick and healthy, wealthy and those in poverty, youth and aged, friend and family, stranger and enemy. All gathered to worship God. They were all sinners moving toward being one people forgiven by the creating God. This gathering is the first component of Christian worship. This gathering of all is counterintuitive in a culture that seems to want to divide people according to gender, race, class, and sexual orientation. These cultural distinctions are important factors shaping our self-understanding and the power and authority structures of society, but they do not determine our standing before God.

As the community entered the sanctuary, members experienced a gathering place that in itself represented a large and inclusive space with vast doors welcoming the whole of creation. Within the sanctuary's oversized walls and vaulted ceiling the imagination could wander in a space of mystery. Its windows surrounded the worshipers with the colorful and textured stories of their ancestors, revealing the pain and suffering of conflict and loss and the grace and freedom of a compassionate and redeeming God. The sanctuary was a haven from the burdened pressure of productive time in the world. The sense of timeless silence and quiet embraced those who gathered so that they could open themselves to the music of their own souls while being held in the music of the faith. It was within this kind of space that the people gathered in procession to practice the liturgy of life and to explore with God the divine vision and direction that will give shape to and empower movement toward the future.

In the church today, the procession—the gathering process—is often less formal and more individualized. Some churches value silence as worshipers enter, and some members enter to vigorous congregational singing, while others engage in conversations of welcome. People walk, drive, and bicycle to the church; some come from nearby and some from far away. Also, the gathering of all in the community has changed to the gathering of those who are more like us. With the Protestant Reformation, the huge umbrella concept of the medieval cathedral standing in the center of the whole community—a gathering place of the rich and the poor, the sick and the well, women and men and children—has changed. We are now more inclined to gather with people who share our economic and social standing and who agree with our beliefs. When there is a conflict, we split off from those with whom we disagree rather than staying together, learning from one another, and helping one another grieve the loss of the world that we might want in order to gain God's realm. Mobility and choice have made it natural to gather with only those like us rather than with all the diverse creatures of God's creation. But the worship of the Divine One of all creation, whose action in Jesus was to redeem the whole of creation, is centered in the gathering of all. This gathering of all, stranger and friend alike, is the core of Christian worship.

The gathering of all becomes the model for Christian living that is practiced in the liturgical experience. Each week people who seek to serve God gather symbolically in their diversity, in their uniqueness, in their rich complexity to worship God. Even though the cathedral space that represents all gathering to worship God has shattered into many churches with many different ways of articulating and living the faith, the echo of that larger reality that sees us as one people with our diverse styles lingers in our worship of the one God in Jesus Christ. This is a reminder to all that each is a creation of the Creator and that each has a place in the community that seeks to serve the Creator.

Father Kavanagh's model medieval gathering included a prayer of confession and an assurance of pardon. (This practice has been moved in some churches and occurs after the liturgy of listening as a way of creating a common basis for our coming together to receive the Lord's Supper.) This ritual practice of identifying our broken and limited human nature was a leveling experience. Forgiveness creates a community of people who know that their presence together is the result of a gracious God whose gift of life is facilitated by mercy. This spirit of forgiveness places grace at the beginning of the journey of discovering our new life in the body of Christ.

The gathering of all for liturgy is primarily a public activity. It is not merely an intimate gathering of friends who simply enjoy the warmth of one another and who feel the Spirit when they are together. Patrick Keifert suggests that it is our culture of intimacy that has hijacked the public nature of worship and that we now expect twenty-first-century Western worship to serve our individual need to feel connected and known. He contends that liturgy is the vehicle by which strangers connect with one another in their common cause of service to the gospel of God in Christ. Keifert writes, "Ritual builds the social barriers necessary for effective interaction. It provides the sense of cover that allows most people to feel safe enough to participate in expressions of religious value. Despite how things may seem when a visitor comes to church for the first time, ritual can in fact be most hospitable to the congregational stranger."[3] We are not a community because we are all nice people who are attractive to other nice people. What creates the church and has sustained it for two millennia has been the gathering of strangers who become connected around their ritual focus on God rather than on their feelings about one another.

By gathering with all to worship God, the mystery of each is affirmed and celebrated. God is more than we can know. God is mysteriously complex and beyond our ability to comprehend. Gathering to worship this mystery reminds us that the others (strangers) with whom we gather are also mystery. They are more than we see or can know. When we explore the mystery of God and experience the adventure and possibility that come from that encounter with the unknown, we are more able to be curious about the rich mystery of others in our church. This ability to be curious is an essential skill for appreciating and navigating differences among people. This ritual practice of gathering with mystery in the Other and in "the others" lays the groundwork for processing conflict and grieving loss. It nurtures the discipline of staying curious. The mystery of the future in the absence of the way things were (when there has been significant change or death within or around the church) becomes the very nature of the faith journey rather than something that should be avoided. Our fear can be moderated as we together remember discoveries we made in exploring the mystery of the Holy and the rich and complex gifts that we have found in our neighbors.

This focus on the gathering of all to worship God, rather than on the gathering of people who like one another, to share a common experience that they can claim is an experience of God, helps form a community that understands that there are differences that are essential to the nature of the church. It reminds people of the theological agenda of this community called "the church," and it can function to help people mentalize their situation when they are at odds with others. It forms the theological base of the ability to access the depressive mode of human behavior that is aware of deep complexity and of mutual pain so that members of the gathered community can remain connected and listening to one another in the midst of difficult conversations around controversial issues that they face together.

Leading a congregation in this liturgical practice requires the leader to constantly remind the gathered community of its diversity and the meaning of that diversity in the worship of God. It is the practice of invitation that is required. Not only do leaders work within the church to share the stories of tradition and to structure the community to move forward into the new world, but the leaders also are out among the people, calling and gathering people to join with all others in worship of the Holy. This gathering and sharing of meaning is not something that is done only in a crisis, but it also is done with regularity throughout the years and decades of formation and reformation of the community of faith. This central understanding of the liturgy and the practice of Christian living embodied in the worship helps the church interpret how to deal with the multiple people not only within the walls of the developing and redeveloping church but also in the community around the church. The neighbors around the church are invited to be one with us rather than objects of either our fear or our service. The practice of the gathering to engage the presence of God in worship is also a reminder to each individual that all parts of the self are also seen as partners in this experience of liturgy and thus in the Christian life. Humans are not just one thing. We are multiple selves whose parts work together, and, in our better moments, those parts can live with some sense of cohesion. But we have within us not only the friendly parts of ourselves that we like; we also have within us the parts of ourselves that are an enemy to the selves we want to be. We have the discordant portions of ourselves that have trouble being welcomed in polite society. We have the greedy as well as the graceful components within ourselves. We have the selfish as well as the self-giving. All are gathered in the worship of God in the liturgy. Worship is not complete when we exile parts of our wholeness to the alleyway in back of the church.

Gathering with all to worship God functions liturgically to shape a community of people that is able to discover strength in the differences of those who have come together and to realize that the witness and ministry of a community of multiple perspectives and assets will offer a more effective and enduring blessing for the world than one that is grounded in a narrow, like-minded perspective of similarity. The ability to bless the world is directly related to a community's capacity to be, as the Apostle Paul said of himself, "all things to all people." The capacity to bear witness to the love of God in a complex and diverse world is directly related to the complexity and diversity of the community that is bearing witness.

Listening

The second liturgical component of classic Christian worship articulated by Father Kavanagh is listening. The church gathers with all to worship God and to listen to Scripture, homily, song, and prayer. In the midst of a world in transition and change in which conflict and loss are constant companions, a sanctuary bathed in silence in which one can listen creates a space for mentalizing and curiosity. The silence that holds the liturgy and weaves itself throughout the wording, singing, and praying of the people is critical to listening for the Divine word. For whatever else one can say about the creation, silence is the most ubiquitous reality. That silence must be honored and embraced, for it is within the vast mystery of silence that words take shape and create meaning. Barbara Brown Taylor puts it this way:

> By addressing the experience of God's silence in scripture and in our listeners' own lives, we may be able to open up the possibility that silence is as much a sign of God's presence as of God's absence—that divine silence is not a vacuum to be filled but a mystery to be entered into, unarmed with words and undistracted by noise—a holy of holies in which we too may be struck dumb by the power of the unsayable God.[4]

Within a sanctuary whose walls are filled with the laughter of weddings and babies and the tears of the wounded and grieving, the community gathers to listen for insight into the Divine agenda for the world and to discover how it might participate in the agenda of this creative mystery. This central component of worship creates people who know that their first activity when they come to worship is to open their ears to the music of the Creator within the gifts of creation. Contrary to what many think about the purpose of the church, the primary agenda of the church is not to speak, but it is to listen. Only when listening is central does speaking on behalf of God become an option.

The leader of the Christian community is not the model for Christian living just in her standing to proclaim something; she is a model fundamentally in her ability to open her ears to the creatures and hear what the Creator might be whispering through those creatures. When the leader listens to the creation, she will discover the diversity of voices and the multiplicity of opinions and commitments. It is this careful and patient listening that contributes to her developing a "heart of flesh." For it is in knowing others that she is affected by who they are and the ways in which they are experiencing the life they live both individually and together. In sharing that life with them, she and the community as a whole are then able to experience at a deep and authentic level their loss and struggle. In sharing that struggle, she can then hold within herself their pain and bring it into relationship with the pain and joy of others to whom she has listened and whom she has gotten to know.

When the leader listens and knows and shares life in this way, she models for others this capacity of listening to others with a heart of open caring—a heart of flesh. When leaders in a church are curious about the creation and are willing to ask those around them questions that will help them discover the presence of the Divine in them, the church (and the world, too, for that matter) will take notice. People who have truly been heard become people who might have a greater capacity to truly hear. Leaders who can model listening and curiosity even about things that may be hard to hear contribute to the developing of a community that can listen even when what members of that community are hearing might be difficult to receive.

As is becoming clear in this discussion of liturgy and preaching, the leader's role is not simply to step out front and lead the gathering of all to worship God. It is also to immerse himself within the community by deep listening and caring. This positions the leader to lead the diverse individuals and groups that gather. A leader isn't one who declares the truth as he sees it, but he listens and discovers the diverse voices of the community and seeks to understand the multiple possibilities that God may be exploring within the church. As he hears, and helps the community hear, those possibilities, he helps the church discern its direction as well as which of the gifts that are present in the church might be used to serve that direction.

When the leader listens this way to those who have gathered, she then speaks with a heart of flesh. This is why pastoral care and preaching are so integrally related. A preacher who listens with warm hospitality to the multiple voices within the community has a hard time being one who declares absolute truths with hard edges. She not only hears the multiple voices of all the diverse people who gather for worship but also hears the multiple voices of the individuals as they negotiate the diverse demands and claims that are in conflict in the homes of their own souls. One who knows the hard work that humans do in order to work out their individual and communal lives will speak with a voice that is filled with sympathy, irony, and tenderness. Assumptions that our own truth is the truth that somehow explains all of life will be moderated in the preacher whose heart is softened by listening well to the gathered community.

The preacher who understands multiplicity and who has the ability to recognize the diversity within all who are gathered before him can also then develop the ability to listen to the multiple voices within the broader community of the tradition that is represented in the Bible and in the community of the saints. The Bible's rich and complex makeup is grounded in hundreds of years of shifting cultural and theological values and of diverse people's struggles with themselves, others, and God within their context. These biblical stories reveal not only conflict within the communities of the faithful but also the diversity of perspective in multiple communities of faith. Preaching that takes the Bible seriously is preaching that reveals the differences, the struggles, the conflicts, the losses, and the blessings of those communities. When contemporary churches understand that they are recipients of traditions that were filled with struggle and tension, they at least know that something is not wrong with them when they are in conflict with one another. They may even be able to live in the hope that just as the church survived its struggles in ancient times, they can survive and flourish through the conflicts of today.

The spiritual leader who listens also preaches with the ability to help each gathered member become acquainted with others and in so doing become connected with the Other. Pastor Marquis failed to reflect this hope of connection when he preached his sermon "God's Call to Our Future" to the members of Urban Chapel when in conflict over whether to build a new sanctuary or a community center. Had he listened and felt the pain of those who disagreed with the building of the sanctuary, he might have approached the topic with more reflection on the multiple possibilities of God's desires. God is in the others around us; and in our ability to lovingly listen, to pay attention with the heart, we discover the Divine. We listen and are in relationship with God and with the other. When we differ with the others in the church, that difference challenges some of what we might hold to be true and causes us to rethink what we know. This rethinking softens the edges of the knowledge and forces us to expand our understanding. When the edges of our understanding are softened, our heart is softened. It becomes more fleshy and less stonelike. This is especially true as we seek solutions to issues that have no clear answers. If God is doing something new, then the directions for the future have not yet been discovered. The sharing of perspectives from different angles and insights will enrich our decision-making processes, improving the chance that our way forward will more likely succeed in its efforts to bless the world.

When we listen and our heart becomes more fleshy, we then become more vulnerable. The laughter and tears of the other reach more deeply into our perspective on the world and on what we and the church ought to be about. Our consideration of the direction of the church is then shaped by the heart of the other that has reshaped our own heart. The decisions that we make are then attentive to the emotions and the thoughts of others. Decisions that determine that we will do one thing and not another will by necessity mean that someone will lose some of what he had hoped for, but if that loss can be experienced within the context of a group of people who understand and appreciate the cost that was incurred by some people in the group, it will be easier to move forward. If those who achieved their goals can do so with an empathic presence with those who did not win the day, the community has a better chance of continuing together than it would if the divided parties fail to comprehend the pain and cost that the other has incurred.

When we gather with all to listen, we hear differently than if we are alone or in a like-minded group of people. When we listen to a story about the Hebrew people wandering in the wilderness as we sit alongside people who have homes and feel relatively secure and self-assured, we hear that story one way. But when we listen to that same story while sitting next to a person who just lost his job and behind another person who just lost her home and in front of a person who is losing his mind to Alzheimer's disease, we hear differently. Wilderness becomes an existential reality within the group even if it isn't something that one person can grasp at that particular point in his life. But his heart is softened by his connection to the others for whom this story is their story.

Within this gathering of all who are listening to one another and who are held together by the liturgical rituals of faith, the preacher can then explore the conflicts and the differences that may be present in the congregation or the community around the church. Guided by a heart that listens and a mind that is curious about how God is working within this multiplicity that is the creation in which she lives, she can wrestle with the issues that need to be worked on. This discernment of direction and decision is not always an easy process, but when the community knows that it is being heard, when it trusts that its diversity is being honored, when people trust that care and thought will be given in the process of discovery, the differences have a better chance of producing better decisions.

We believe that this stance in the pulpit would have contributed to a less contentious conflict within the Urban Chapel. Instead of striding into the pulpit and delivering a sermon in which he declared that God had shown him the future and that God desired the people to build a new sanctuary, Pastor Marquis could have approached the issue with acknowledgment that this is a difficult decision to make. He could have revealed the struggle that people of God have in discerning Divine direction. He could have shared several sermons over a few weeks in which he explored the diverse opinions and how they represented what could very well be considered Divine insight. He could have shared stories from the Acts of the Apostles in which people were in conflict with one another in trying to discern how the church of Jesus Christ might move forward with the guidance of the Holy Spirit. By extending the time of discernment and sharing the struggles within the liturgy and the sermons, Pastor Marquis could have helped the people work through the possible solutions and revealed respect for the diverse opinions even though not all opinions would prevail. This kind of preaching contributes to the creation of a community of conversation in which all are heard and in which all opinions are given due consideration.

A preacher with "a heart of flesh" is one who, in the empathic presence with the congregation, develops a voice that reaches below the mind and into the heart and soul. The preacher has a responsibility not only to hear the divine Other in the presence of others but also to articulate and give voice to the deep yearnings

140

of the heart as it engages the deep wonder of mystery. For humans to assert themselves within creation, they need to be grounded in the grand silence of that creation. But in that silence, in relationship to all creation, they are called upon to assert their own voice to affect the emerging shape of reality. When a preacher is shaped by a heart of flesh, she discovers what Mary Donovan Turner and Mary Lin Hudson call her "authentic voice." She speaks in a way that "extends the presence of truth between persons in relationship, allowing the truth to surface where it will and to do its work in the lives of those who allow it."[5] And she must speak:

> To remain silent is to fail to acknowledge our value as human beings made in the "sound" of God. To remain silent is to prevent ourselves from being "known" and, therefore, being part of the life-giving conversation with others. To remain silent is to deny the continuing creativity of God to draw "new worlds" into the present and future moment.[6]

A preacher who speaks out of this deep empathy becomes a healing presence among people who are struggling to navigate life with its tensions and conflicts and helps them draw on the deep presence of mystery to sustain them in their journey.

Making Offering

The third leg of the liturgical journey that shapes the community's life is that of making offering. We gather with strangers to worship, and in that context we listen and hear the heart of the Divine who comes in multiple ways, sometimes creating conflict that results in our stonelike hearts being formed into flesh. It is then those hearts of flesh—hearts that suffer the vulnerability and pain of loss and grief—come together to make themselves an offering to God who is worshiped. This offering is symbolized by bread and wine, symbols of God's suffering heart with the creation and with the gifts of our labor as we break ourselves and give ourselves piece by piece to life and to the ministry of the church. The Eucharist is the gift of the people, brought in their incomplete and broken spirit and transformed by God's creative presence into food for the soul with which to bless the fragmented world. When the broken and divided self joins with others who share that state of brokenness and offer themselves to the service of the God who seeks to reform the world in a more just and loving way, the energy of their joint offering can be changed into strength for grieving the losses of life. In this grieving, the church and the world become more open to the creative hope of the new world that God is creating.

This shared process of grieving within the boundaries of the eucharistic experience contributes to the healing of the soul by its memorializing activity. To remember the broken Jesus is to put one's self in a place of remembering our own traumatic breaking. To remember is to reexperience the trauma of one's own suffering. Within the Eucharist we are held by the suffering and pain of Jesus while we rework our own trauma and loss and discover the new that might emerge from it. If the past is not remembered, as painful as it might be, those events can continue to live in the psyche and can create resistance in the effort to move forward into the new reality. Laurence J. Gould, in his work on memorialization, shares the story of how Germans needed to remember and work through their relationship to the Third Reich before they were able to move toward reconciliation. This working through was facilitated by the process of creating memorials at the sites of death camps that represented the atrocities possible when humans lose their way.[7] Within the ritual practice of the Eucharist, Christians are invited to revisit their losses, their brokenness, and their alienation to reexperience the pain and suffering that they once knew and to work it through so that it will not control their future. They are invited to do this work together with others who are also reworking their own lives and discovering that remembering their experiences well can free them from the power of the pain so that they might have energy to embrace the future.

Within this component of the liturgy, we are able to pour our whole selves into the community. The Eucharist invites us to offer our vulnerability and our agency to the One who is working to create a more just and loving world. In this practice the church is affirming that it is where people come with all that they are and that God is desirous of that all for the purpose of blessing the world. Each person is unique. Each person has particular and different aches and tears. Each person has been broken in different ways. Each person has unique assets of strength to share. Each person has been given gifts of the Spirit to bless the whole. Too many times the church excludes the gifts of some by honoring the gifts of a few. The church seems more interested in the gifts of teaching than they are in the gift of tears. Churches seem to honor those with money more than they honor poverty. Churches encourage persons to bring their time and give it to building a habitat house but are not sure what to do with someone whose fears keep them from acting to protect themselves from the abuse of others. But when all come together to worship God and all listen for God, then all are invited to bring their unique offerings and present them so that they can be transformed into gifts for the blessing of the world.

The ritual liturgical practice of the Lord's Supper is designed for all people—those who are in the center of life and those who are marginalized—to come together and experience the hospitality of God. In his discussion of the conflict in the church at Corinth, Patrick Keifert reports that some were interested in making the meal a private matter for those who were on the inside:

> The tendency (perhaps natural) to privatize the meal had to be rejected because it gave lie to the central claim of the gospel, namely, that in God's self-giving, self-sacrificing presence in this meal, a new humanity—even a new cosmos—was being made. Thus, the Eucharistic meal was not to begin before all were given a chance to gather. The inclusion of those on the periphery and the ordering of the community's table fellowship quite against ordinary structures of social life were essential to the gathering.[8]

Thus, leaders in the liturgical practices of the church are responsible for ordering life in such a way that all have an opportunity to be present in worship.

Leaders who are responsible for gathering all for worship guide the people to name and offer their unique gifts for the service of the common ministry of the church. After guiding the discernment of gifts, leaders can help people determine which gifts can be offered to that end. The gifts of some will need to be held for a while and will not be able to be used in each ministry. Leaders help the community remember the multiple gifts so that they may be offered at a different time for the good of the whole. Thomas's doubt is a gift that is available for the community of the disciples, but sometimes doubt needs to be set aside, and Peter's certitude is what is required. At other times the questions of a doubter are critical for discerning a future that is best for the church. Leaders help the community pick and choose which gifts are appropriate for which time and place.

This offering and matching of gifts and needs is important for a community that is learning to deal with conflict. People's different perspectives and gifts are offerings. They are all important, even if they are given by people who are not liked very much. Gifts are to be honored. It may be that some gifts are diametrically opposed to one another within a given set of conflicts or issues. If these are gifts from God, the leaders must help the church find ways to hold those gifts and to allow them to emerge again in a time when they might be important for the church's moving forward into the future.

When our gifts are not received in a given conflict, we must learn to grieve that loss. We must learn to live without that which we value. In this learning to live we will learn from the experience of being alienated from what we know to be true and good. We will discover that we continue to live while contributing to the breaking of relationships and the hurting of self and others. But by remembering and reworking our lives within the context of the containing grace revealed in God's actions toward the world, we know ourselves to be loved by God and thus are free to explore and make mistakes, confess our error, and receive forgiveness that freedom for the future might flourish. In other words, we participate in what Serene Jones calls sin: "Sin describes human life that is not oriented toward God, life that does not unfold in full knowledge of God's love and desire for the flourishing of creation."[9] The practice of the Eucharist is the practice of hope that death and loss are not the final word in God's scheme and that the sin in which we participate does not capture and hold us in the past. Breaking ourselves and giving ourselves to the holding of the broken and self-giving God binds us together with Divine energy and hope. Even when we have failed to have our gift of understanding and insight prevail in a given conflict within the church, it does not mean that the gift is useless or undervalued. It is held and becomes part of the story of the people, shaping and reshaping the community as it goes forward.

Departing in Peace

The fourth component of the liturgical practice of the Christian community is the experience of departing in peace. Christians gather to practice the virtues of the faith as they gather with all to worship God by listening deeply for the Divine and, in response, by making themselves as an offering to God. But the purpose of the Christian faith isn't just to create communities that gather to find blessing for themselves. The purpose of the gathering is for the blessing of the world. Until the church moves beyond the walls of its gathering to live in the world with hearts of flesh instead of hearts hardened by fear and greed, we have not completed the liturgy. The transformation of groups within the church is for the sake of the transforming of the world loved by God.

This transforming dimension of the liturgical experience is one of agency. Participating with all who gather in listening for God's word and in sharing the symbols of breaking and transformation functions to infuse the participant with energy for action that blesses the world. The symbols that shape our understanding and our hope for a new reality are symbols that might help others in the world claim the abundance of life that is available to them. All too often, people discover that the central symbols of their lives fail them. Joseph M. Webb remembers a book by Kenneth Burke titled *Permanence and Change: An Anatomy of Purpose.*[10] For years Webb taught it to his students and helped them discover what he calls their "hub symbols." He contends that we are, as individuals and as organizations, created by the symbols that are at the center of our self-understanding. One's orientation to life is a "tangle of words, names, terms—all with whatever emotional charges we have picked up from the variety of people and places during our growing-up years—all of this symbolic mix must be organized so that it will, at least within us as individuals, 'hang together,' as it were."[11] These "hub symbols" are often challenged in these rapidly changing times. The practices of Christian gathering with strangers and listening for the Divine word in the midst of the vast silence of what some might define as emptiness are the gifts that we bring to the world to help it discover new "hub symbols" by which to orient life. With the symbols of offering that represent the breaking of life and the sharing of it in a community of remembrance, Christians offer the people in the world a place where they can discover and speak symbols that do not deny the reality of a frightening and broken world but that give them hope that, in acting with courage to grieve their losses, they might wake up to a new world of grace and opportunity.

Leaders offer direction in this liturgical move by being out in the community themselves. They take their offering of a broken and blessed self and become a gifted presence in the family and workplace. They involve themselves in civic discourse and contribute their insights in the political considerations of the larger community. This presence helps reveal to others that the engagement of diverse voices in the world can enrich the body politic and form a richer and more complex community of blessing.

Challenging the people to move outside the walls of the church and continue their worship by the blessing of their community is central to the practice of Christian living. The struggle at Urban Chapel was intense precisely because the church knew itself as a people whose liturgical practices moved from the sanctuary into the streets. Ultimately, the Urban Chapel moved through its conflict and was able to make its move into a new sanctuary because some of the leaders made a decision that the transition into a new worship space would not diminish the church's commitment to the work with those who lived in the neighborhood. They created a new not-for-profit organization that solicited funds not only from church members but also from other churches and philanthropies to renovate an old discount store building into a community center. This building became a center for a new inter-denominational ministry that expanded Urban Chapel's witness into a community ministry. Leaders who had wisdom to explore different and diverse ways to respond to need were able to remain connected with those who felt that they had lost the struggle over the building of the new sanctuary.

Leaders also pay attention to the losses that people experience when they have participated in the larger community and have had to sacrifice something they valued in that participation. When leaders struggle outside the church with the same issues as those of the community of faith, they are more effective in their empathetic support of their parishioners. The sharing of the breaking of their hearts in the chaos of the civic world contributes to their maintaining hearts of flesh as they lead their members in issues of justice and peace.

This practice of the liturgy is a constant reminder to those who gather that there is a reason to work out the differences. The conflicts that are part of being human and are central to being Christian are present not because something is wrong with the church but because of our human diversity. When held within the sanctuary of the liturgy, conflicts can become the energy and vitality of the creative Spirit of the Divine who desires that the human community develop ways to bring together those diverse and complex differences in a way that the gifts of each can contribute to the blessing of all. Leaders in the church who have been working with communities of difference and listening deeply have received as a gift hearts of flesh. Those leaders have helped develop communities of people who can receive the diverse gifts of God and discover ways of working so that those gifts come together to bless all. Those people then become the leaven for the earth, to bless the world and help it move toward more just and loving ways of being.

The practice of liturgy and preaching gives language and stability to a community that is called to constant change as it seeks to serve a creative God in a recreative mission of evolving love and blessing. Leaders who are open to the gathering of all, who are sensitive to those who are left out, and who listen to the diverse and multiple voices of God in the gathering of the strangers help create space in which differences might be processed. When such leaders help a community discern the activity of the Divine in the church, they then guide the decisions to determine which gifts are to be offered at which time in the community. They help hold the community together at the table of offering and lead the people from the sanctuary into the streets where peace is offered to the world.

Final Comments

Conflict is an inevitable dimension of human life. It is not inherently sinful—far from it. Rather it is an expression of life in community in which difference is real and not (thankfully) finally eradicable. Whatever else it is or might become, conflict is a sign of life, passion, interest, and concern. It is part of the destructive/creative ordering of the world. It is a gift of God, one might say, that like all such gifts can be profoundly misused and mistaken. In the Christian faith, it finds its natural home in the liturgical rhythms of life together. Leadership in conflict, therefore, is ultimately liturgical leadership: an effort to live our conflicts with one another in the midst of the life-giving sanctuary of the covenant. The sanctuary becomes a place where grief and hope can sometimes be known in their depths—can be enacted long enough and richly enough within the ongoing liturgy that is our corporate and personal life to make space for something new.

The liturgy invites us amid it all to participate more fully with God's own struggle, to learn from experience, and to lean sometimes breathtakingly into God's efforts to actualize God's own desires for love and justice in the world. The adventure of faith in the midst of conflict demands a willingness to risk beyond what we are comfortable risking. Living fully into and through the liturgy is not for those who need to have their own way, who cannot tolerate their favored ways of construing the world turned upside down, or who cannot at least in promise strive to grieve what is impossible to grieve.

We will fail in part, of course, even at our best. Our fragility and our sin will make sure of that. Our best conflict resolutions resolve only in part, not in full. The liturgy lives in the shadow of the "not yet" even as it resides in the "already." In the words of Barbara Brown Taylor with which we began this book:

> Our words are too fragile. God's silence is too deep. But oh, what gorgeous sounds our failures make: words flung against the silence like wine glasses pitched against a hearth. As lovely as they are, they were meant for smashing. For when they do, it is as if a little of God's own music breaks through.[12]

And in that music, we may hear the driving visceral rhythms and the enchanted, mystical tones echoing from the depths of it all that call us back, as in the liturgy itself, to begin again in humility and courage the hard work of learning from our experience as a community how to live faithfully with broken hearts of flesh.

Notes

1. Leading in Conflict: An Introduction to the Issues

1. For an overview of some of this literature, see K. Brynolf Lyon, "Issues in Congregational Conflict," *Quarterly Review* 23, no. 1 (Spring 2003): 97-103.

2. Erik Erikson, *Insight and Responsibility* (New York: Norton, 1964), 47-80.

3. James M. Burns, *Leadership* (New York: Harper and Row, 1978), 18.

4. Ibid., 19.

5. Robert Klein, Cecil Rice, and Victor Schermer, *Leadership in a Changing World: Dynamic Perspectives on Groups and Their Leaders* (Lanham, MD: Lexington Books, 2009), 119. See also Simon Western, *Leadership: A Critical Text* (Los Angeles: Sage Publications, 2008); Laurence Gould, Lionel F. Stapley, and Mark Stein, eds., *The Systems Psychodynamics of Organizations: Integrating the Group Relations Approach, Psychoanalytic, and Open Systems Perspectives* (New York: Karnac Books, 2001); and Edward Shapiro and A. Wesley Carr, *Lost in Familiar Places: Creating New Connections between the Individual and Society* (New Haven: Yale University Press, 1991).

6. Klein et al., *Leadership in a Changing World*, 3. See also the discussion of Kenneth Eisold, "Leadership and the Creation of Authority," in *Group Dynamics, Organizational Irrationality, and Social Complexity: Group Relations Reader 3*, ed. Solomon Cytrynbaum and Debra A. Noumair (Jupiter, FL: A. K. Rice Institute for the Study of Social Systems, 2004), 289-302.

149

7. Klein et al., *Leadership in a Changing World*, 2. See also the essays in Clare Huffington et al., eds., *Working Below the Surface: The Emotional Life of Contemporary Organizations* (London: Karnac Books, 2004).

8. The classic works applying family systems theory to congregations are those by Edwin Friedman. See especially his *Generation to Generation: Family Process in Church and Synagogue* (New York: Guilford, 1985), and *A Failure of Nerve: Leadership in the Age of the Quick Fix* (New York: Church Publishing, Inc., 2007). We will discuss these more fully later in chapter 4.

9. Joseph Folger, Marshall Poole, and Randall Stutman, *Working through Conflict*, 6th ed. (New York: Allyn and Bacon, 2008).

10. See the essays in Cytrynbaum and Noumair *Group Dynamics*.

11. For perspectives that make this connection especially clear, see Vamik Volkan, *Killing in the Name of Identity: A Study of Bloody Conflicts* (Charlottesville, N.C.: Pitchstone, 2006); Cynthia Burack, *Healing Identities: Black Feminist Thought and the Politics of Groups* (Ithaca, N.Y.: Cornell University Press, 2004); and Martha Stark, *Working with Resistance* (Northvale, NJ: Aronson, 1994).

12. Dan Moseley, *Lose, Love, Live: The Spiritual Gifts of Loss and Change* (Nashville: The Upper Room, 2011), 27.

13. Ronald Heifetz, Alexander Grashow, and Marty Linsky, *The Practice of Adaptive Leadership* (Boston: Harvard Business Press, 2009).

14. Thomas Tweed, *Crossing and Dwelling: A Theory of Religion* (Cambridge: Harvard University Press, 2006).

15. Zygmunt Bauman, *Liquid Modernity* (Cambridge: Polity Press, 2000), 1-15.

16. Ibid., 13-14.

17. Ibid., 14.

18. To explore more fully how leadership spans across boundaries, see Chris Ernst and Donna Chrobot-Mason, *Boundary Spanning Leadership: Six Practices for Solving Problems, Driving Innovation, and Transforming Organizations* (New York: McGraw Hill, 2011), 5.

19. See Anton Obholzer and Sarah Miller's discussion of the importance of staying on task in "Leadership, Followership, and Facilitating the Creative Workplace," in *Working Below the Surface: The Emotional Life of Contemporary Organizations*, 33-37).

2. Failing to Find What We Didn't Know We Needed: Three Stories

1. The distinction we are after here overlaps with that of Ronald Heifetz's discussion of adaptive versus technical challenges and Otto Scharmer's discussion of "learning from the future as it emerges." See Ronald Heifetz, *Leadership without Easy Answers* (Cambridge: Belknap, 1994) and C. Otto Scharmer, *Theory U: Leading from the Future as It Emerges* (San Francisco: Berrett-Koehler, 2009).

2. Jaco Hamman, *When Steeples Cry: Leading Congregations through Loss and Change* (Cleveland: Pilgrim Press, 2005); Gerald A. Arbuckle, *Change, Grief, and Renewal in the Church: A Spirituality for a New Era* (Westminster, MD: Christian Classics, 1991); Howard Stein, "Letting Go of Who We Were: The Triad of Change-Loss-Grief in Organizational and Wider Cultural Life," *Organizational and Social Dynamics* 6, no. 2 (2006): 204-23.

3. Richard R. Osmer, *Practical Theology: An Introduction* (Grand Rapids, MI: Eerdmans, 2008).

4. Don S. Browning, *A Fundamental Practical Theology: Descriptive and Strategic Proposals* (Minneapolis: Fortress, 1991)

5. Peter Homans, *The Ability to Mourn: Disillusionment and the Social Origins of Psychoanalysis* (Chicago: University of Chicago Press, 1989).

6. Martha Stark, *Working with Resistance* (Northvale, NJ: Aronson, 1994), xii.

7. Ibid., 123-25. See also Irwin Z. Hoffman, *Ritual and Spontaneity in the Psychoanalytic Process: A Dialectical-Constructivist View* (Hillsdale, NJ: Analytic Press, 1998).

8. From the perspective of psychoanalytic thought, see, for example, Vamik Volkan, *Killing in the Name of Identity*; Cynthia Burack, *Healing Identities*; K. Brynolf Lyon, "Companions on the Way: Creating and Discovering the Congregational Subject," *Encounter* (Winter/Spring, 2002): 147-57; and Howard Stein, "Letting Go of Who We Were."

9. See David Wallin, *Attachment in Psychotherapy* (New York: Guilford, 2007).

10. Wilfred Bion, *Experiences in Groups* (London: Routledge, 1961). See also Earl Hopper, *Traumatic Experiences in the Unconscious Life of Groups* (London: Jessica Kingsley, 2003), 146-53.

3. Taking and Being Taken by a Role: Getting Askew and Getting Aright

1. For the fuller complexity of Luther's position, see the classic study by Gustaf Wingren, *Luther on Vocation*, trans. Carl C. Rasmussen (Eugene, OR: Wipf and Stock, 1957).

2. Larry Hirschhorn, "The Psychodynamics of Taking a Role," in *Group Relations Reader 2*, ed. Arthur Coleman and Marvin Gellar (Washington, DC: A. K. Rice Institute, 1985), 336.

3. See, for example, Charles Taylor's massive and powerful study of these issues in *A Secular Age* (Boston: Belknap Press, 2007).

4. Larry Hirschhorn, *The Workplace Within: Psychodynamics of Organizational Life* (Cambridge: MIT Press, 1988). See also his *Reworking Authority: Leading and Following in the Post-Modern Organization* (Cambridge: MIT Press, 1997), 57-70.

5. Hirschhorn, "The Psychodynamics of Taking a Role," 338.

6. Ibid., 343.

7. Jon G. Allen, Peter Fonagy, and Anthony Bateman, *Mentalizing in Clinical Practice* (Washington, DC: American Psychiatric Press, 2008).

8. See Hirschhorn, *Reworking Authority*.

9. For those unfamiliar with the technical language of psychoanalytic thought, one of the best overviews of self psychology remains Ernest Wolf, *Treating the Self* (New York: Guilford, 1988).

10. See, for example, Phillis Isabella Sheppard, *Self, Culture, and Others in Womanist Practical Theology* (New York: Pallgrave Macmillan, 2011); and Robert Randall, *Pastor and Parish: The Psychological Core of Ecclesiastical Conflict* (New York: Human Sciences Press, 1988).

11. Thomas H. Ogden, *The Primitive Edge of Experience* (Northvale, NJ: Jason Aronson, 1989).

12. Wilfred R. Bion, *Experiences in Groups and Other Papers* (London: Tavistock, 1961); and Earl Hopper, *Traumatic Experience in the Unconscious Life of Groups* (London: Jessica Kingsley, 2003).

13. When Hirschhorn speaks of "social defenses," he means things in addition to basic assumption behavior in the Bion sense. For our purposes, however, we are going to focus solely on basic assumption behavior.

14. Hopper, *Traumatic Experience in the Unconscious Life of Groups*, 36.

15. The classic texts remain those of Edwin Friedman. See note 8 of chapter 1.

16. A good overview is Elizabeth Howell, *The Dissociative Mind* (Hillsdale, NJ: Analytic Press, 2005).

17. Phillip Bromberg, *Awakening the Dreamer: Clinical Journeys* (Hillsdale, NJ: Analytic Press, 2006).

18. For a related discussion, see Hirschhorn, *The Workplace Within*.

19. In Elliot Jaques's classic description, "a role may be defined as a knot in a social net of role relationships. A role stands not on its own feet, but only in relation to other roles with a connection between them," in *A General Theory of Bureaucracy* (New York: Halsted, 1976), 25.

20. For a fuller discussion, see K. Brynolf Lyon, "Scapegoating in Congregational and Group Life: Practical Theological Reflections on the Unbearable," in *Healing Wisdom: Ministry in Depth*, ed. Kathleen Greider, Deborah van Deusen Hunsinger, and Felicity Kelcourse (Grand Rapids, MI: Eerdmans, 2010).

21. Earl Hopper, *The Social Unconscious: Selected Papers* (London: Jessica Kingsley, 2003).

22. See, for example, K. Brynolf Lyon, "Uses of Otherness in Group Life: Racism, White Privilege, and Christian Vocation," *Encounter* 68, no. 1 (2007): 19–32; Kathy Kram and Marian Hampton, "When Women Lead: The Visibility-Vulnerability Spiral," in *The Psychodynamics of Leadership*, ed. Edward Klein, Faith Gabelnick, and Peter Herr (Madison, CT: Psychosocial Press, 1998); Janice M. Steil and Liora Hoffman, "Gender, Conflict, and the Family," in *The Handbook of Conflict Resolution: Theory and Practice*, ed. Morton Deutsch, Peter Coleman, and Eric Marcus (San Francisco: Jossey-Bass, 2006), 223-240.

23. Donnell B. Stern, *Partners in Thought: Working with Unformulated Experience, Dissociation, and Enactment* (New York: Routledge, 2009), 10.

24. The phrase "calm and courageous no matter what" is borrowed from the subtitle of Peter Steinke's Friedman- and Bowen-inspired *Congregational Leadership in Anxious Times: Being Calm and Courageous No Matter What* (Herndon, VA: Alban Institute, 2006).

25. In addition to Steinke's text noted above, see also Walter Mischel, Aaron DeSmet, and Ethan Kross, "Self-Regulation in the Service of Conflict Resolution," in *The Handbook of Conflict Resolution* (see note 22), 294-313.

26. John D. Caputo, *The Weakness of God: A Theology of the Event* (Bloomington: Indiana University Press, 2006).

27. Our thanks to our colleague Helene Russell for pointing out the Augustinian analogy.

28. See, for example, Lee Butler, *Liberating Our Dignity, Saving Our Souls* (St. Louis: Chalice Press, 2006).

4. *Failing to Grieve and the Spiritual Discipline of Learning from Experience*

Chapter 4 is an expansion of K. Brynolf Lyon, "The Hatred of Learning from Experience," *Encounter* 61, no. 4 (Autumn 2000): 465-78. Used by permission of *Encounter*.

1. See, for example, Don Browning, *A Fundamental Practical Theology*. Also, Martin Jay, *Songs of Experience: Modern American and European Variations on a Universal Theme* (Berkeley: University of California Press, 2005).

2. Clark Williamson and Ronald Allen, *The Teaching Minister* (Louisville, KY: Westminster John Knox, 1991), 7.

3. See also Anthony G. Banet and Charla Hayden, "A Tavistock Primer," in *The 1977 Handbook for Group Facilitators*, ed. J. E. Jones and J. W. Pfiffer (San Diego: University Associates, Inc., 1977); and R. L. Munich, "Varieties of Learning in an Experiential Group," *International Journal of Group Psychotherapy* 43, no. 3 (1993): 345-61.

4. See Wilfred Bion, *Experiences in Groups and Other Papers* (London: Routledge, 1961). See also Thomas Ogden's discussion in "Bion's Four Principles of Mental Functioning" in *Rediscovering Psychoanalysis: Thinking and Dreaming, Learning and Forgetting* (New York: Routledge, 2009).

5. Ronald Heifetz, *Leadership without Easy Answers* (Boston: Harvard University Press, 1998).

6. For a helpful discussion of learning from experience in feminist theology, see Kristine A. Culp, " 'A World Split Open'? Experience and Feminist Theologies," in *The Experience of God: A Postmodern Response*, ed. Kevin Hart and Barbara Wall (New York: Fordham Press, 2005), 47-64.

7. See Isca Salzberger-Wittenberg, Gianna Williams, and Elsie Osborne, *The Emotional Experience of Teaching and Learning* (London: Karnac Books, 1983).

8. See Melanie Klein, *The Selected Melanie Klein*, ed. Judith Mitchell (New York: Free Press, 1986).

9. See J. D. Lichtenberg, *Psychoanalysis and Motivation* (Hillsdale, NJ: Analytic Press, 1989); Joseph D. Lichtenberg, Frank M. Lachmann, and James L. Fosshage, *A Spirit of Inquiry: Communication in Psychoanalysis* (Hillsdale, NJ: Analytic Press, 2002); and Adam Phillips, *The Beast in the Nursery: On Curiosity and Other Appetites* (New York: Vintage, 1999).

10. See Jonathon Lear, *Open-minded: Working Out the Logic of the Soul* (Cambridge: Harvard University Press, 1998).

11. In postmodern theology, see especially the work of John Caputo. See his *The Prayers and Tears of Jacques Derrida* (Bloomington: Indiana University Press, 1997), and his *The Weakness of God: A Theology of the Event* (Bloomington: Indiana University Press, 2006).

12. Heifetz et al., *The Practice of Adaptive Leadership*, 96 and 152.

13. Tim Harford, *Adapt: Why Success Always Begins with Failure* (New York: Farrar, Straus, Giroux, 2011), 253-54.

14. Sigmund Freud, "Mourning and Melancholia," in *Standard Edition* 14, trans. James Strachey (London: Hogarth Press, 1957), 243-60.

15. Kristine Culp, *Vulnerability and Glory: A Theological Account* (Louisville, KY: Westminster/John Knox, 2010), 181.

16. See Salzberger-Wittenberg et al., *The Emotional Experience of Teaching and Learning*; and Donald L. Finkel and William R. Arney, *Educating for Freedom: The Paradox of Pedagogy* (New Brunswick, NJ: Rutgers University Press, 1995). See also Richard Billow, *Relational Group Psychotherapy: From Basic Assumption to Passion* (London: Jessica Kingsley, 2003).

17. See W. Clark Roof and William McKinney, *American Mainline Religion: Its Changing Shape and Future* (New Brunswick: Rutgers University Press, 1987).

18. John Caputo, *What Would Jesus Deconstruct? The Good News of Postmodernism for the Church* (Grand Rapids, MI: Baker, 2007), 30.

19. See Larry Hirschhorn, *Reworking Authority*. See also L. Gregory Jones, "Forgiveness," in *Practicing Our Faith: A Way of Life for a Searching People*, ed. Dorothy C. Bass (San Francisco: Jossey Bass, 1997). An interesting discussion focused more generally may be found in Alina Tugend, *Better by Mistake: The Unexpected Benefits of Being Wrong* (New York: Riverhead Books, 2011).

20. See Paul Fiddes, *The Creative Suffering of God* (London: Routledge, 1992).

21. See Robert J. Schreiter, *The Ministry of Reconciliation: Spirituality and Strategies* (Maryknoll: Orbis Books, 1998).

22. See Edward Farley, *Divine Empathy: A Theology of God* (Minneapolis: Fortress Press, 1996).

23. Alfred North Whitehead, *Process and Reality, Corrected Edition*, ed. David Ray Griffin and Donald W. Sherburne (New York: Free Press, 1978), 351.

24. Culp, *Vulnerability and Glory*, 159-81.

25. See Erik Erikson, *Insight and Responsibility* (New York: Norton, 1964).

26. Serene Jones, *Trauma and Grace: Theology in a Ruptured World* (Louisville, KY: Westminster John Knox, 2009), 151-65.

27. Jesus' deep irony here is drawn from Matthew 11:30 and Matthew 19:21.

28. Joseph S. Nye Jr., *The Powers to Lead* (Oxford: Oxford University Press, 2008).

29. This discussion draws on the wonderful work of Martin Jay, *Songs of Experience.*

30. Martin Jay, *Songs of Experience*, 6-7. See also the helpful conversation of Richard Bernstein, *The Pragmatic Turn* (Malden, MA: Polity Press, 2010).

31. See Martin Jay's discussion of James in *Songs of Experience.*

32. Experience as the site where "neither binary dualisms nor reductive monisms rule out the experimental moment in living" is developed by Martin Jay, *Songs of Experience*, 404. For a fuller discussion of certain of these issues as they relate to practical theology in general, see Helene Russell and K. Brynolf Lyon, "Positioning Practical Theology: Diversity, Contextuality, and Otherness," *Encounter* 72, no. 1 (Spring 2011): 11-30.

5. *Shaping the Congregational Journey: Losing Your Way to New Life*

1. Recent studies in organizational change reveal similar factors that must be at play when processing group conflicts. See James Krantz, "Dilemmas of Organizational Change: A Systems Psychodynamic Perspective," in *The System Psychodynamics of Organizations: Integrating the Group Relations Approach, Psychoanalytic, and Open Systems Perspective*, ed. Laurence Gould, Lionel F. Stapley, and Mark Stein (New York: Karnac, 2001), 133-56.

2. For an extensive exploration of the issue of saving face, see Folger et al., *Working through Conflict*, 174-202.

3. Zigmunt Bauman, *Liquid Times: Living in an Age of Uncertainty* (Cambridge: Polity Press, 2007), 3.

4. J. William Worden, *Grief Counseling and Grief Therapy*, 4th ed. (New York: Springer, 2008).

5. Sigmund Freud, "Remembering, Repeating and Working Through," in *Standard Edition* 12 (see note 14 in chapter 4), 147-56.

6. Jane Pooley, "Layers of Meaning: A Coaching Journey," in *Working Below the Surface: The Emotional Life of Contemporary Organizations*, ed. Clare Huffington et al. (London: Karnac, 2005), 182.

7. Ibid., 183.

8. Harford, *Adapt: Why Success Always Begins with Failure.*

6. Preaching and Practicing Liturgy: Resources for Leading Congregations in Conflict

1. Dan Moseley, *Lose, Love, Live: The Spiritual Gifts of Loss and Change* (Nashville: The Upper Room, 2011).

2. Aidan Kavanagh, *On Liturgical Theology* (New York: Pueblo Publishing Co., 1984).

3. Patrick R. Keifert, *Welcoming the Stranger: A Public Theology of Worship and Evangelism* (Minneapolis: Fortress Press, 1992), 110.

4. Barbara Brown Taylor, *When God Is Silent* (Cambridge: Cowley Press, 1998), 18.

5. Mary Donovan Turner and Mary Lin Hudson, *Saved from Silence: Finding Women's Voice in Preaching* (St Louis: Chalice Press, 1999), 11. For a rich and fascinating exploration of the role of listening and speaking from the perspective of finding voice among women in ministry, read this book.

6. Ibid., 52.

7. Laurence J. Gould, "Collective Working Through: The Role and Function of Memorialisation," *Organisational and Social Dynamics* 11, no. 1 (Spring 2011): 79-92.

8. Keifert, *Welcoming the Stranger*, 69.

9. Jones, *Trauma and Grace*, 102.

10. Kenneth Burke, *Permanence and Change: An Anatomy of Purpose* (Berkeley: The University of California Press, 1954).

11. Joseph M. Webb, "When the Center Doesn't Hold: A Working Orientation for Pastors Dealing with Transition and Crisis," in *Transitions: Leading Churches through Change*, ed. David Mosser (Louisville, KY: Westminster John Knox, 2011), 220.

12. Barbara Brown Taylor, *When God Is Silent*, 121.